HELP!

I'M LOCKED UP...AND CREATED FOR SO MUCH MORE!

HELP!
I'M LOCKED UP...AND CREATED FOR SO MUCH MORE!

LYNN POTTER

Potter's Heart Ministry

Ministering God's love to the broken.

HELP! I'm Locked Up... and Created for So Much More!

by Lynn Potter

Published by Potter's Heart Ministries

ISBN 978-1512170931

Cover design by Brenda Haun, www.brendahdesigns.com

Cover image from ©gmddl / Fotolia

IN HONOR OF BILL, BONNY,
AND
LAZY B'S RANCH...

WHERE AWESOME KIDS
ROAM

Dedication

Infants crawl and reach with wonder in their eyes at every new discovery.
Toddlers never give up trying to walk no matter how many times they fall.
Children laugh, play, and dream, saying, "Someday, I'll..."

Destiny is in our bones. It's part of our makeup. It is the driving force that causes mankind to never stop its quest for greatness and discovery. We've gone from communicating by drawing pictures on cave walls to high-speed internet, from travelling by horse and buggy to jet airliners. *Every child is born for greatness. Every child is created by God to walk with Him into their destiny.*

Sadly, many hopes and dreams die. Many destinies are buried under the rubble of life. Jesus made a remarkable statement in Mark 10:14. He said, "Let the little children come to Me, and do not forbid them, for of such is the kingdom of God." He was correcting His followers because they thought the children were bothering Him. Jesus' response to their view was…

He took them (the children) up in His arms, and blessed them. (Mark 10:16)

No matter what life has thrown our way, there is still an infant, toddler, and child in every one of us. We are still crawling, reaching, and dreaming of *Someday, I'll….*

As I said before, it's in our make-up. God created us this way. The problem is that life happens. Things come our way to steer us off course. *This book is dedicated to those who have lost their way, and want to do something about it.*

Sit back, and relax, as Alex and Hillbilly share their story of lost dreams, hope, and restoration. Walk with them. Learn from them. Find out how they overcome. Read with that infant, toddler, and child inside of you coaching you along the way.

Do as Alex, Hillbilly, and those little children did so long ago...come to Jesus and receive His blessing over your life because...

**YOU WERE
CREATED FOR SO MUCH MORE!**

Contents

Introduction

"Hey Hudson, you should write a book."

"Hillbilly, I don't know the first thing about writing a book."

"That don't matter, Hudson. God does..."

Hillbilly's simplicity never ceases to amaze me. God uses it to get my attention, and jump-start me into what I am supposed to be doing. I am an avid reader, and love books. But, I *never* saw myself *writing one!* That is, at least, not until now.

"Oh, Hillbilly...I don't know. What would I write about?"

"Us, Hudson...our story..."

* * *

You hold in your hands the fruit of Hillbilly's simplicity, and God's miraculous power to change a life and its destiny. It is our gift to you. I trust you will find hope and healing as you journey with us through our ups and downs.

As I tell you our story, I will be pausing every so often to invite you to a *fireside chat*. These *fireside chats* will give you an opportunity to reflect on some key points in our story, examine your own life, and journal your thoughts.

I have to laugh as I remember the end of my conversation with Hillbilly. You will understand what I'm talking about after you get to know him. It went something like this…

"Yeah, Hillbilly, you're probably right…"

"No probably about it, Hudson. I *know* I'm right."

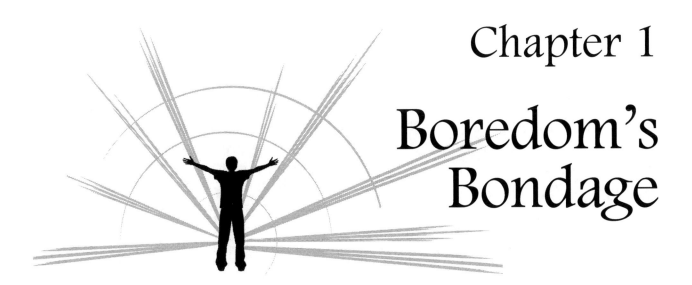

Chapter 1

Boredom's Bondage

It's cold and damp outside, which adds to my ongoing disgust. I've been summoned to jury duty, and I can think of a million other places I'd rather be. It doesn't help that it's just a degree or two above freezing, so who knows what it'll be like by the time I get out of the courthouse.

I enter the old building and find the sign outside the jury room inviting me…no… ordering me to take a seat. Now, if you've never had the privilege of being called to jury duty…well…let's just say…good for you.

It's day two and we're still choosing jurors. I've not been excused yet, which is a surprise to me, but then again, you never know. Word on the street is Carlucci's on the hot seat for this jury. I heard he's coming up against some pretty heavy charges, but my sources aren't the greatest. Most of the time, all they do is stir up drama with stories they invent while on a bad trip.

They call their drama inventions stretching the truth, but from what I remember, there was *never any truth* involved. But, just for the record, I hope they're right, and I get the satisfaction of watching Carlucci squirm.

Ms. Madeline dropped me off with the promise she'd come get me as soon as I called her. I got my license back, but still don't have any wheels, so she's got to take me just about everywhere…that is, unless it's in walking distance, and I feel like hoofing it.

I've been out (of prison) for several years now, and my employment situation *still* has not improved. I can find part time work, but it never lasts. Most of the time, I'm just living paycheck to paycheck, barely able to help Ms. Madeline pay the bills.

Granny's college fund for me is long gone, so we are just about out of options. It's a real temptation to revert back to my old ways of making a living, but I can hear Granny screaming in the background, *Alex...don't!!!* So, I just wait, and wait some more, still *dreaming* of *getting a life* someday.

Ms. Madeline's voice fades, and some *very evil* thoughts take its place.

I suppose jury duty has a positive side to it...it is something *different*...an unpleasant change from the *boredom* that threatens to consume me. It's pretty sorry when you choose jury duty over *anything*. So, from my point of view, *boredom is lower than the pits*. In fact, when I look back through the years, I'm pretty certain *boredom* is what caused me to get locked up most of the time...in the beginning anyway.

As I sit in my assigned seat, I think about what Ms. Madeline said before she drove away. "Alex," she said. "You really ought to go back to *The County* and volunteer again. It might just get you out of the slump you're in. You were doing so well, and I know Granny would've been real proud of you. Wouldn't it be better than sitting around watching re-runs on T.V. all day? Didn't you get enough of that when *you* were locked up?"

"I don't know, Ms. Madeline. It didn't seem to make much of a difference. I kept seeing the *same faces* over and over...like nobody listened to a word I said. Guess I saw a lot of myself in there, and didn't like what I saw. Maybe I'll go back someday...just not right now."

"OK. Suit yourself. But, I know you wouldn't be *so bored* if you were doing something positive, instead of moping around all day. Trouble's just lurking around the corner you know...waiting to pounce on that *bored-emptiness* you carry around everywhere you go. Even Elsie knows something's wrong with you, and she's a dog. I'm worried about you, Alex. Just watch yourself...please."

Ms. Madeline's voice fades, and some *very evil* thoughts take its place. I shake my head, willing them to go away. If I wasn't in this courthouse *waiting for something to happen*, I could very well be on my way to *making something happen*, that could cause me to get into some serious trouble. I was bored before I got here, and, if it's even possible, I'm getting *more bored* every minute I have to sit here and wait for something to happen.

Maybe Ms. Madeline's right. I need to get it together, and stop wandering around, and doing nothing, or I'll end up doing more time. I could be sitting in the hot seat facing the judge and jury myself. And, you know, I've done *that* more times than I'd like to admit. I'm thinking about taking Ms. Madeline's advice, and rethinking my position. But, not today, I just got too much on my mind.

As I look around the room, I see one of Granny's church friends, and try to hide by slouching down. I don't need some old lady coming over to me, fussing around. I'm just not in the mood.

I still can't figure out why I'm here. I didn't think people *like me* were even *allowed* to be on a jury. I'll look into that when I get home if they don't dismiss me today. Other than my desire to see Carlucci take a hit in the system, there's nothing that attracts me to this place.

I scan the room to see if there's anyone else I know. When you come from a small town like Apple Grove, you're bound to know someone just about anywhere you go. And, if you're like me, and you've been in the paper more than once, that substantially adds to the list of potential privacy invaders.

I spot one of my old COs, (Correction's Officer) and memories of what *went down* the last time we had an encounter resurface. *It was me*. I ended up on the floor because I had been shot with a hit of mace after I started a pretty heavy fight in our block. He was the one stuck with preparing me for *another* trip to *the hole*. I wasn't the most cooperative person, even in my restrained state, to say the least. I gave it my best shot at being a pain in the a-- through the whole thing, and was told so by numerous people after they let me out. That was a long time ago, and he might not remember. But, just in case I'm mistaken, I look the other way to avoid any eye contact.

The chatter in the room is maddening. I wonder how long I'll be stuck here before they find out who I am, and politely tell me the *likes of me* are not wanted. I hope it happens soon, because, believe me, the disgust is mutual.

The courtroom is musty. It has that *old building* smell to it, the smell that makes you feel like you're in a sauna, with dust crawling up your nose. And, if that's not bad enough, the windows are covered up so there's very little light in the place. It's hard enough to stay awake with all the droning going on; they could at least let some light in. I feel like I'm trapped in a dark, dirty cave, and couldn't be more miserable if I tried. Giving in to the mandatory torture, I zip up my jacket, lean back, and *impatiently wait for something to happen...*

"HUDSON, ALEXANDER..."

The guy next to me leans over, pokes me in the shoulder and says, "Hey sleeping beauty, your prince is calling." He rattles the magazine he's reading, and coughs.

I wonder how long I've been out. I'm slouched so far down in my chair that my butt's numb, and I'll be lucky if my back isn't curved for life. I turn toward this dream-destroyer and say, "Yeah? What's it to you?"

"Hey, man. Don't get so hot. I don't want to be here anymore than you do, just trying to hurry things up, is all."

I pull myself up and make my way out to the isle. We are crammed in rows of ten chairs each and I ended up in the middle. Don't you just hate that? I do.

Anyhow, I'm walking up the isle toward the front, and someone behind me whispers, "Hudson, that you? It's me, Sandusky. Where you been?"

I don't answer, turn, or respond in any way. This provokes another try, "Hudson... C'mon Alex...where you been?"

I keep walking. This is *not* a good thing. Sandusky and me, well...let's just say, we don't need to be in the same country, let alone the same room. We spent a lot of time together, if you know what I mean. Our addresses had more numbers attached to them than you could imagine. And, when we weren't *locked up* together, we were better off at least a hundred miles apart...with no tangible means of communication. I haven't seen him in years.

Sandusky taught me all I needed to know at an early age about how to maintain a level of *high-class living* with little or no work involved. "Kid," He'd say. "You stick with me and you'll never have to worry about nothing. I got your back. You just keep doing what I say. You'll see. No never mind your Ma and Pa are gone. You got me now. And, don't worry about Granny. What she don't know won't hurt her."

Just hearing Sandusky's voice starts a whole new set of memories to surface. You can't believe what a voice will do. It can bring back people, places, and things that are better left buried at the bottom of the deepest sea. Between trying to ignore Sandusky's voice, and the anticipation of hearing anything about Carlucci's case, my mind is in overdrive.

I didn't think people *like me* were even *allowed* to be on a jury.

A bailiff comes toward me and escorts me out of the room. "Mr. Hudson, it is not the intention of this court to embarrass anyone, but you are disqualified for service. You are excused." With an understanding nod, I say, "Yes sir, thank you sir."

We walk back into the room, and I make my way toward the back door that leads out to E. Liberty Street. This is where Ms. Madeline agreed to pick me up. But, I'm *really not* into listening to another one of her lectures about my lack of motivation, so I'm not going to call her.

I need to clear my head and process what just happened. I still want to find out what goes down with Carlucci, but need to stay out of it until it hits the papers. There's too much history with him I don't want to resurrect.

And…Sandusky…man, that's just too creepy for comment.

I need to walk, get some fresh air, and clear my head. I'm just about out the door when I hear Sandusky's name called. I'm sure he's going to get the same treatment I did. What I can't figure out is…how did he ever get a legit license to end up in the jury pool? Well, none of my business, any of it. And, the sooner I get away from this place, the better…

Fireside Chat
Boredom's Bondage

Well, there you have it...my day in court as a potential juror...and my expulsion.

I'm not in a very good place right now...you know what I mean? I'm not talking about what's going on *around me*. (Although, it certainly has contributed to the intense conflict I'm experiencing.) I'm talking about what's going on *inside of me*.

> **No one gets through this life without experiencing the boredom battle at some time or another.**

On the surface, it really doesn't look *that* bad. It's just a lousy day and *I'm bored*. But, deep down inside, there's a fierce battle going on between light and darkness. I call it the **boredom battle**; the battle for my future. If I stand my ground and light wins, all is well. If I don't, darkness wins, and I'm in *big trouble*.

I have an idea you know what I'm talking about. No one gets through this life without experiencing the *boredom battle* at some time or another. As I tell my story, I'll be stopping every so often to give us a chance to step back, and take a look at what's going on. It's my way of sharing with you what I've learned about this life-and-death battle, and how we can win the fight for our future.

Through fighting many of these **boredom battles** myself, I've come to understand some very important things. If I remember them, they come to my rescue when I'm just about to head down a direction I need not go. I would strongly suggest you make them part of *your* understanding...

1. Boredom is a powerful force that can lead us into one of two directions.
2. The power behind this force is either **destiny-driven** or **darkness-driven.**
3. Both have the ability to control our lives, and ultimately our future.

4. God has created us with the free will to choose which power we embrace.
5. *Darkness-driven boredom* will drive you away from God and His purpose for your life. It is a powerful tool the devil uses to strip us from our true identity, and entice us into doing things we were never meant to do.

Your ultimate destruction is its goal.

Destiny-driven boredom will bring you closer to God and His purpose for your life. It is a powerful tool God uses to draw us to Himself, in order to show us who we are, and what we are meant to do.

Your divine destiny is its goal.

Darkness-driven boredom is *a selfish, vicious taskmaster*. It prowls around like a rabid wolf ready to pounce and devour. It searches for someone who will do its dirty work for short-lived, empty rewards. It has the ability to take a lousy, boring day, and turn it into a life-changing night of horror. It uses *fantasy-driven* rewards to get us into its clutches.

The main goal of darkness-driven boredom is to entice us into doing things we were never meant to do, thus <u>steering us away from</u> our God-intended purpose and future...

DARKNESS-DRIVEN BOREDOM WILL BE REPLACED WITH EMPTY PROMISES AND DEATH.

On the other hand...

Destiny-driven boredom is a kind, wise, unselfish guide. It leads with gentle prodding, willing the best for us at all times. It offers a future filled with excitement, fulfillment, and purpose. Destiny-driven boredom has the ability to take a lousy, boring, day, and turn it into a life-changing *new beginning*. The rewards of destiny-driven boredom are peace, contentment, and a sense of well-being.

The main goal of destiny-driven boredom is to lead us into what we are created to be and accomplish, thus <u>steering us into</u> our God-intended purpose and future...

DESTINY-DRIVEN BOREDOM WILL BE REPLACED WITH FULFILLMENT, PURPOSE, AND LIFE.

* * *

Well, my friend, that's it...my take on boredom and what it can do. At first I thought I was way out in left field with these thoughts, that is, until I started taking a look at what was happening to me...

These truths have saved me from disaster more than once. Fill in the blanks below. You will find the answers on the previous two pages.

Explain what a ***boredom battle*** is:

_____

_____

List the 4 things we need to remember about *boredom* that will help us stay out of trouble:

  1. _____

  2. _____

  3. _____

  4. _____

Darkness-driven boredom will _____ His
_____ for our lives. It is a powerful tool the devil _____
_____ and _____
Our ultimate_____ is its goal.

Destiny-driven boredom will _____ and His
purpose for our lives. It is a powerful tool God _____
_____. Our _____ is its goal.

Darkness-driven boredom is a _____, _____.
It prowls around like _____.
It searches for _____
_____. It has the ability to _____
_____.
It uses _____ to get us into its clutches.

_____

10

The main goal of *darkness-driven boredom* is_____
_____, thus,
steering us away from _____.

Darkness-driven boredom will be replaced with _____ and _____.

Destiny-driven boredom is a _____, _____, _____.
It leads with _____, willing _____.
It offers a future filled with _____, _____,
and _____. Destiny-driven boredom has the ability to
_____.

The rewards of destiny-driven boredom are _____, _____,
and a sense of _____.

The main goal of *destiny-driven boredom* is to lead us _____
_____, thus steering us _____
_____.

Destiny-driven boredom, will be replaced with _____,
_____, and life.

Here's the deal. There are two beings who are after our lives...our Creator God, and the destroyer, the devil. It's *our choice* who we give our lives to.

WE ARE VALUABLE AND MOST WANTED. OUR LIVES MATTER, AND HAVE PURPOSE. WE ARE GIVEN THE CHOICE TO CHOOSE WHERE WE END UP, AND WHO TAKES US THERE!

Before we move on, fill in the blanks with your name, then write the entire state-ment out using your name. Say it out loud after you are finished; declaring it over your life....

I, _____, *AM VALUABLE.*
I, _____, *AM MOST WANTED. MY LIFE MATTERS.*
I, _____, *HAVE PURPOSE.*
I, _____, *AM GIVEN THE CHOICE TO CHOOSE*
WHERE I, _____, *END UP AND WHO TAKES ME THERE.*

Write the previous statement out on the following lines, using your name:

_____

_____

_____

_____

_____

_____

_____

_____

Read the above statement out loud three times.

Read the following verse, and write it out on the lines provided:

Ephesians 2:10: For we are His workmanship, created in Christ Jesus, for good works, which God prepared beforehand that we should walk in them.

_____

_____

_____

Write Ephesians 2:10 out using your name:

For I, _____ am His workmanship, I, _____
am created in Christ Jesus for good works, which God prepared for me,
_____ beforehand that I, _____
should walk in them.

Read the following verses from the Bible, God's Word, and write them out on the lines provided. Then, write what you feel they are saying *to you, about you:*

Ephesians 2:10: For we are His workmanship, created in Christ Jesus for good works, which God prepared beforehand that we should walk in them.

_____

_____

God's Word is telling me in Ephesians 2:10 that I:

_____

_____

_____

Psalm 139:13-15 From the Life Recovery Bible: You made all the delicate, inner parts of my body and knit me together in my mother's womb. Thank you for making me so wonderfully complex! Your workmanship is marvelous-how well I know it. You watched me as I was being formed in utter seclusion, as I was woven together in the dark of the womb.

_____

_____

_____

_____

_____

_____

God's Word is telling me in Psalm 139:13-15 that:

_____

_____

_____

Jeremiah 29:11-13: For I know the thoughts that I think toward you, says the Lord, thoughts of peace and not of evil, to give you a future and a hope. Then you will call upon Me and go and pray to Me, and I will listen to you. And you will seek Me and find Me, when you search for Me with all your heart.

_____

_____

_____

_____

_____

God's Word is telling me in Jeremiah 29:11-13 that:

_____

_____

_____

_____

_____

_____

Jeremiah 1:4-5 From the Life Recovery Bible: The Lord gave me this message: "I knew you before I formed you in your mother's womb. Before you were born I set you apart and appointed you as my prophet to the nations."

_____

_____

_____

_____

God's Word is telling me in Jeremiah 1:4-5:

_____

_____

_____

_____

_____

_____

John 10:10: From the Life Recovery Bible: The thief's purpose is to steal and kill and destroy. My purpose is to give them a rich and satisfying life. (Jesus is talking about the devil (the thief) and Himself in this verse.)

_____

_____

_____

God's Word is telling me in John 10:10:

_____

_____

Before our parents ever knew each other, we were wanted, loved, cherished, and set apart for greatness in the heart of God. He watched over us as we were being formed. He thinks _good things_ about us. There _is no love_ like our Creator God!

We are created with specific _purpose_ and _destiny_ by
Our _Creator_ who _loves_ and _cherishes_ us!!!

OK...so, what does all this have to do with anything? Let's take a closer look at what's going on in my life...

Things aren't going well, I'm somewhere I don't want to be, I am *bored*, and my past shows up out of nowhere. Look out!!! These four things are a *recipe for disaster.* I am being set up for failure. I am being set up for destruction.

Boredom is on the prowl, has found me, and wants to keep me from my destiny by sidetracking me into doing things I was never meant to do. It wants to team up with my lack of motivation, my past, and my most recent rejection…being excused from jury duty.

I am *ripe for disaster* because I have been weakened by life's circumstances, and *boredom* will try to tempt me to do something I was never meant to do.

Fill in the blanks from the previous paragraph:

1. Things aren't _____.
2. I'm somewhere _____.
3. I am _____.
4. My past shows_____.
5. I am being _____ for failure.
6. I am being set up for d_____.
7. Boredom is on the _____, found me, and wants to keep me _____ by _____.
   _____.
8. I am ripe for disaster because _____
   _____
   _____.
9. Write about a time in your life where you believe *darkness-driven boredom* was enticing you into doing something you were *never meant to do.*

_____
_____
_____
_____
_____
_____
_____
_____
_____
_____
_____

What was the outcome of this *darkness-driven boredom* event?

_____

_____

_____

_____

_____

Re-read what I've shared with you about my day in court in Chapter 1, and list below all the negative things that were happening to me and around me. Explain why you think I was in such a *bad place*.

_____

_____

_____

_____

_____

Write about a time in your life where you were in a bad place...a place that you would consider a *recipe for disaster,* and yourself *ripe for disaster.*

_____

_____

_____

_____

_____

_____

What was the outcome of this bad place you just wrote about?

_____

_____

_____

_____

_____

_____

ALWAYS REMEMBER...

> *Boredom, when darkness-driven,* will keep you from your destiny
> by sidetracking you into doing things you were never meant to do.

Re-read and write out the verse below. This is the *foundation* of our study. We will be referring to it often.

For we are His workmanship, created in Christ Jesus for good works, which God prepared beforehand that we should walk in them. Ephesians 2:10

_____

_____

_____

When we are *bored,* our minds want to *rescue us.* They try to fill the *boredom* with *fantasy. Fantasy* is a powerful tool that darkness uses to get us to do things we know are wrong. *Fantasy is a cunning artist. It paints pictures that look beautiful but are deadly. It is a seductive master. It produces feelings and bodily responses that are false, leaving us empty and ashamed. It is a thief and liar. It steals our innocence, and lies to us in the process.*

Fantasy's main goal is to KILL US and uses BOREDOM to CON us into its clutches.

FANTASY IS NOT REAL
FANTASY STEALS AND LIES
FANTASY IS DESTRUCTIVE AND DEADLY

FANTASY IS THE DEVIL'S COUNTERFIET OF GOD'S CREATIVE IMAGINATION

Before we go any further with our story, I want to give you a chance to look at your life and what part *boredom* has played in getting you into trouble. Write about a time where you were totally *bored,* and did something that got you into trouble. What were you thinking? How did fantasy play a part? What were the *mental images* that came, and how did you react to them? Did you hear suggestions along with seeing mental images? What was the outcome? Dig deep into the situation. Use extra paper if needed.

_____

_____

_____

_____

_____

Personalize Ephesians 2:10 by writing your name on the lines provided. Read the statement several times in order to become familiar with what it says *about you*.

I, _____ am His workmanship, created in Christ Jesus for good works, which God prepared beforehand that I, _____ should walk in them.

There are four truths in this verse that will change the course of our *bored, fantasy-driven* lives into *exciting destiny-driven lives,* if we will embrace them....

1. We are His workmanship.
2. We were created in Christ Jesus for good works.
3. God created these good works for us ahead of time.
4. These good works were created so that we would walk in them.

First, let's take a look at the word ***workmanship*** from our verse in Ephesians, and see if we can get a better understanding of who we are, and why ***boredom*** and ***fantasy*** are such dark enemies.

Workmanship comes from the Greek word *polema,* said like: poy-ay-mah. *Polema* comes from the verb *poieo,* which means *to make, create.* Similar to our words poem and poetry, ***workmanship,*** or polema, gives us the idea that *we are* a created poem or poetry. Used in the above verse, it implies ***we are God's poetry.***

Our poetic lives are a <u>beautiful thing</u> when they are *destiny-driven* by <u>God.</u> They <u>become destructive</u> when *fantasy-driven* by *boredom.* Let me explain:

Poetry expresses the thoughts, emotions, and deep feelings of the author. Poetry can move its reader emotionally, spiritually, and physically. It can war against injustice, create passions in others, and make statements through words.

List two ways our lives can be driven and the result:

1. _____-diven by God   result: _____
2. _____-driven by boredom   result: _____

There are three things you must have to write a poem someone can read. You need an *<u>author,</u>* a *<u>writing instrument,</u>* and something to *<u>write on.</u>* For the sake of this study, God and the devil are the *authors,* The Holy Spirit, or demonic spirits are the *writing instruments,* and our lives are what are being *written on.* <u>We are the *paper*</u>.

List 3 things we must have in order to write a poem someone can read:

    1. An a_____
    2. A wr_____
    3. Something to _____

Who are the authors we have been given the free-will to choose from to write our life stories?
    1. _____
    2. _____

What are two kinds of writing instruments we may encounter?
    1. The H_____Spirit
    2. dem_____spirits

    It is our choice who the author is, and what type of writing instrument the author uses. We have been given the free-will to choose by our Creator.

Is your life **boredom-bound** or **destiny- bound**? Who is the author of your life? What do people experience when they read its poetry?

Please take a few minutes to answer the following questions. It is my suggestion that you take your time, and *think seriously* about what they are asking. Be honest with yourself, and use extra paper to write down your thoughts.

What is your definition of *boredom*?

_____

_____

Have you ever made bad decisions because you were bored? Y____ N____

Do you do what everybody else does because you can't think of anything better to do? Y____ N____

Do you take things that don't belong to you for the thrill of it? Y____ N____

Do you look for excitement in drugs, alcohol, sex, because you are bored? Y___ N___

Do you dream of being rich and try to find ways to become rich without working? Y___ N___

Do you know why you are on this earth? Y___ N___

Does your life seem to have any meaning? Y___ N___

Do you seek fulfillment in things you know are wrong? Y___ N___

Do you wonder what your purpose is? Y___ N___

Do you want to know what your purpose is? Y___ N___

Do you care about anything? Y___ N___

Do you care about anyone? Y___ N___

Who do you think is writing your poem (your life)? God_____ Devil_____

Why? _____

Right now my life is: *boredom-bound*   *destiny-bound* (circle one)

Explain your answer: _____

_____

_____

_____

_____

_____

_____

Right now I believe   *God   the devil*   is writing my poem, or   *Both God and the Devil*   are writing my poem. (Circle one)

Explain your answer _____

_____

_____

_____

Let's review what we have learned so far... *We are His workmanship...*

We are God's *workmanship.* Explain on the following lines what *workmanship* means as it relates to your life:

_____

_____

Our lives are like poetry. What does this poetry express?

_____

_____

What 3 things must we have to write a poem?

_____

We choose who will write our poem, our life story...the choices are:
The d_____ or G_____

There are 2 spirits who are the writing instruments. They are:
The H_____Spirit or d_____ spirits.

On the following lines, explain what kind of poem your life has become, who is writing the poem, what instrument is being used to write it, and why you feel this way...

_____

_____

_____

_____

_____

_____

_____

_____

_____

_____

_____

Now, back to our story...

Chapter 2

Rescue's Revelation

Apple Grove's courthouse is dead center of town. It sits on the corner of Courthouse Boulevard, (imagine that) and Main St. Why they call it Courthouse *Boulevard* is beyond me. The speed limit is 15mph, and the road dead-ends at Old Hillbilly's barn. I scan the *boulevard* with increasing disgust...a slow road going nowhere...

Anyhow, it's still miserable outside, weather wise, and to tell you the truth, it's pretty miserable inside; that is, inside my head. I can't shake the thoughts of Sandusky and all we've been through. Mental images of our past play in my mind like a bad movie in a dark, dingy theater. They are about to make me go stark-raving mad. I shake my head as I descend the courthouse steps, praying they'll go away.

The sidewalk needs repair, as much of this town does. The storefronts have seen better days, but people still mill around as though they don't notice. There are a few old ladies coming out of Karen's Kitchen across the street, chattering. I gasp as I watch them jaywalk without looking. There's a loud honk as a truck rounds the corner, and almost flattens them.

Where's the news crew? I laugh out loud. This would be the most exciting thing that's happened here in a long time. I can see the headline now...*Old Ladies Flattened as Pickup Truck Rounds Corner.* Wow...I got'a get a life.

I probably *should* call Ms. Madeline, and let her know I'm walking home, but she'll go on and on about how I should let her come get me. She'll whine about how I might run into somebody I'd be better off not seeing, or be tempted to do something I shouldn't do.

When's she going to get off my back? She's worse than Granny ever was.

I'm almost at the railroad tracks where Apple Grove's *Historic Train Station* stands. I say that with a twist of sarcasm. It's been abandoned for years, and has gigantic boards nailed across every door and window. The only thing historic about it is its age. Talk of renovation is brewing, but, I say, good luck.

I shiver as the bitter cold wind blows a piece of paper across the street.

Sullivan's Cadillac/Mercedes dealership is the first place you pass after the train station. Sandusky and I *worked* there *on occasion*, if you know what I mean. One of those *jobs* got us locked up for a couple years.

I shiver as the bitter cold wind blows a piece of paper across the street. I pull my coat collar up as far as it will go. It's freezing, and the skies are that gunmetal gray that adds misery upon misery to this miserable day.

Sure could use a shot of something! Anything to liven up this unbelievably useless day!!! Might warm my insides too…

I watch as a lone stray cat crosses over the tracks, and, for a very short, extremely sick moment, I imagine a train barreling down the tracks with lightning speed, and my heart rate increases…I have entered the ***dark side of boredom.***

I shake my head willing the grotesque image to stop.

Think, Alex, think. Think of something good…something admirable…something positive. C'mon Alex, you can do it!

The battle in my mind rages. I *cannot* think of *one positive thing* about today…

The sky's gray, the trees are bare, it's freezing, and I am SO bored!!! Nothing to do but go home and veg in front of the TV…nothing to do but go home and listen to Ms. Madeline drone on about everything. I'm about to flip out, I'm SO flippin BORED!!!! Good thing I don't have any money, Haley's upscale pub is right around the corner. Bunch of stiff shirts hang out there, though. White collar crime- types, drinking all day, because they got too much money and time on their hands...

Granny's voice enters...*C'mon Alex...remember the day you went over to the park and hooked up with those thugs? Remember what you told me as the Sheriff came to my house the next day? Remember???*

This battle in my mind is interrupted by a barking dog. I keep walking, trying to ignore the ear-piercing noise. This causes him to bark louder, and I hear him choke as he enters attack mode. I turn around. He's chained to the building with two bowls flipped over nearby. Must have been his food and water bowls... there is a sick-looking pile of mush trampled under his feet.

I scream at the dog. "Rover, get over it, Rover. SHUT UP!!!" I have no idea what his name is, but at the moment, Rover works. I walk over to the chained-link fence to see what he will do. At least an encounter with him might break the monotony of the day. I take my boot off despite the blistering cold, and drag it across the fence. He shows his teeth, and paces back and forth as I antagonize him. This excites me. I am in control, *making something happen.* I find sick enjoyment messing with him. I told you, I'm entering the dark side of boredom.

I laugh at the insanity of my actions, and for a split second, I make plans to enter the gate. *See if you can get past him to that Eldorado over there! Bet you can! Bet you can do better than that! Bet you can start the thing, and drive right on out'a here with it. Go ahead. You'll be out'a here 'fore Rover knows what hit'em.*

Done it before!!! I know you haven't forgotten how, or lost your touch...

Hey, what 'bout Sandusky back there? You know y'all are the best when it comes to joy riding in something that ain't yours!!! C'mon, Alex! This once ain't gon'a hurt one thing. You owe it to yourself to see if you still got it in ya! Go ahead!

AT LEAST YOU WON'T BE SO FLIPPIN' BORED!!!

Rover's snarling, and I smile. I'm getting into the fact that I'm able to cause this animal to salivate. He's pulling with all his might, and choking himself on the gargantuan chain that barely holds him to the building. What I don't realize is, that old man Sullivan's built himself a house behind the dealership with surveillance cameras, and hears Rover going off.

All of a sudden an alarm sounds, drowning out Rover's barking, and he immediately lies down. Flood lights startle me, and I panic. *You're in big trouble Hudson, if you don't split now.* I high tail it out of there, still holding my boot, which causes me to trample through the miserable slush, soaking my left foot. I'm trying to shove the boot on and run at the same time. It is *not* working.

"Who's out there!?!? I got you on tape, and the Sherriff's on His way, you no good snooping S.O.B...where are you? Don't you worry, we'll find you...you'll rot in the old house upstate, you can be sure...not like in the old days...no sir! I got your number now!!!" Old man Sullivan's voice fades as I run up the hill, and head over toward Hillbilly's place.

I figure I can hide out in Hillbilly's barn for a couple hours then head on home. Ms. Madeline has no idea I've been dismissed. And, what she don't know won't hurt her, now, will it? I don't have to worry about anybody hitting the barn this time of day. I know Hillbilly's schedule...it's been the same for over twenty years.

I look at my watch. It's his afternoon nap time, and everybody knows to stay clear. No partying during Hillbilly's nap time...it's just a long-standing barn rule. It's not really a nap; it's more like *crash time* to give his body some rest before the evening's dose of partying.

At any rate, I'm not violating the sacred rule, just borrowing space until I feel it's safe to be out on the street again. Maybe Sullivan was bluffing, maybe not. Just can't take the chance. I'm praying I had my head down while the camera was on.

I find a spot in the far corner of the west wing of the barn. It's cold and damp, but I don't think anyone will look for me here. Even the law knows Hillbilly don't let anyone in here this time of day. There's a filthy-looking blanket rolled up in a ball under a pitchfork that's leaning against Harrison's stall. Harrison was one of Hillbilly's horses...named him after George Harrison of *The Beatles*. Harrison kept Hillbilly busy and clean, that's until he colicked and died.

Hillbilly took it pretty bad…he went around nobody, and nobody was allowed around him. He sat in this barn for days at a time, with Harrison's blanket wrapped around him, chugging down moonshine he brewed in the back woods with the make-shift still he whipped up.

I tried to talk some sense into him, but Harrison's death put him over the edge. He threw out anyone who tried to come around. He didn't care if he lived or died. I'm surprised he didn't drink himself to death. I have an idea this blanket is Harrison's. It stinks, but it'll keep me from freezing to death, like Harrison almost did.

There's a whole bunch of *party paraphernalia* everywhere, and I choose to ignore it by pulling out my pocket New Testament. I carry it with me everywhere I go, and I know for a fact that it's saved my back side more than once. Today will be no exception, I'm sure. *This is a very dangerous place for me to be bored.*

There's a whole bunch of party paraphernalia everywhere, and I choose to ignore it by pulling out my pocket New Testament.

It falls open to Ephesians 2:10… (Life Recovery Bible)

For we are God's masterpiece. He has created us anew in Christ Jesus, so we can do the good things he planned for us long ago…

I pull the blanket up over my ears and lean back against a bale of hay. I shift my body to make the most of a miserable situation, scan the barn, and start an internal, one-sided conversation with Hillbilly…

Look Hillbilly…I got busted the first time in my life right over there… petty stuff… underage drinking. Why? Cause I WAS BORED. I WAS BORED, Hillbilly, BORED. And, what happened??? Then I got BORED with drinking… I moved on to smoking… I'm talking smoking anything and everything anyone would hand me…

Yeah…and that wasn't enough. I WAS BORED doing all that SMOKIN' and DRINKIN' so I had to be DOING SOMETHING while doing all that SMOKIN' and DRINKIN' !!! Crazy stuff, Hillbilly! Crazy stuff. Yeah…started by stealing that goofy kid's bike… remember? Yeah…that goofy kid owns half of Tri-City Bank and Loan now. He went on to college for four years, and I went on to prison. Now, who do YOU suppose the goofy one really was?

And Hillbilly...what about the women? What about all those innocent girls I took advantage of??? How many kids I got roaming the streets I don't know about? And, you know what, Hillbilly? That WASN'T ENOUGH either!

*Man! Life is **so much more** than looking for a higher high, because you know what??? IT NEVER HAPPENS!!!! No matter what high you're on, it's NEVER HIGH ENOUGH!...*

No matter what high you're on, it's NEVER HIGH ENOUGH!

whether it's drugs, booze, sex, taking risks, stealing, social status, job status...whatever...IT'S NEVER ENOUGH! Look at me! I KNOW BETTER! I almost got caught in the "I'M SO BORED" quicksand again today! ALMOST!!!

The joint... it's calling me again...Hillbilly...

It's saying...C'mon Hudson...you know you want to do SOMETHING CRAZY ...get your heart racing again...it's been way too long, Hudson...you're missing out, man!

You know where to go, who to find...GO ON! Hudson! YOU DESERVE IT!!! Go back... check out Sandusky...see what he's been up to...bet he's NOT BORED!!!

You know what, Hillbilly? It's NOT going to get to me this time, Hillbilly. It's NOT.

And, I'm going to stay here until you wake up. I don't care how mad you get at me. I'm going to try talking to you again. You've got to get out of this life, Hillbilly. You're so much more than a day-to-day drunk, a junkie with nowhere to go. You're so much more than a supplier of the latest high, and a place to make it happen. You're SO MUCH MORE, Hillbilly! I KNOW IT...remember Triple H, Hillbilly? Remember?

Here I am wrapped up in Harrison's blanket. Hillbilly, he wouldn't want you to be like this! He would want you to be free. Free as when you and he used to trot through life together. Hillbilly, Harrison is dead... but he wants you to live.

I'm going to try again... my long time friend...

Maybe...just maybe...that's why God allowed me to experience this unbelievably miserable, bore of a day...maybe it's why I landed up here...

* * *

It's been the same for Hillbilly every day for over twenty years. I tried to talk to him after I finished my last prison gig, but he wouldn't listen. Says all my mumbo jumbo about God and Jesus is just craziness; that I've done too many drugs in my time, and I've lost my mind. Well...maybe so...but I've lost my mind to Someone Who cares about me, and wants to see me succeed in life.

Yeah...a couple hours in Hillbilly's barn just might do me some good. I need a place where nobody knows where I am so I can get back on track. I'm praying my head off right now that nothing shows up on those tapes of old man Sullivan's... if they even exist...

I read the life-giving words again and drink them in like a wondering nomad in the desert who just found an oasis...

Ephesians 2:10:

For we are God's masterpiece. He has created us anew in Christ Jesus, so we can do the good things he planned for us long ago. (Life Recovery Bible)

Jesus, You really are my best Friend. You come to my rescue every time. You watch over me, and intervene just before I make choices that would get me into serious trouble. Thanks for shocking me at old man Sullivan's. (And, yes, I'm working on calling him Mr. Sullivan. With Your help, I can change my attitude!)

I'm going to hang out here until Hillbilly wakes up. Maybe today he will listen and give his life to You. Please, Jesus, only You know how much more abuse his body can take. Please help me reach him! Please help me show him how much he means to You, and that You created him for so much more than he's experiencing in life.

I look toward the door and notice a sliver of sun shining through a crack in the wall. I follow it as is lights up the words on my lap...

For we are God's masterpiece...

Hillbilly...yea...we were God's masterpieces all these years...and we never knew it.

Fireside Chat
Rescue's Revelation

Heading for the joint was my only option, if I continued down the darkness-driven boredom trail laid out in front of me. Thankfully, I was rescued by my Creator God and given His revelation...His insight into what was really going on.

I call it *Rescue's Revelation*.

Can I talk to you just like I've been *trying* to talk to Hillbilly? When I look at him, I wonder how much longer he's going to live if he continues doing what he's doing. Either he's going to get some bad stuff that takes him out, or someone's not going to like the stuff he gives them, and they take him out. Either way, he's done.

That's not what worries me the most. Here's the bigger concern...if he's snuffed out...where's he going?

How about you, friend? You may not be harboring an addictive life in the confines of a barn wasting your life away, but where are you? What are you doing? Where are you headed when your life is over?

What is my point? I'll make it real simple...

ARE YOU READY TO MEET GOD IF YOU SHOULD DIE RIGHT NOW???

WELL?

ANSWER ME...PLEASE...BEFORE WE MOVE ON...

_____ YES _____ NO _____ NOT SURE

There was a time, not too long ago, if you had asked me that same question, I would have had to answer NO or NOT SURE. It wasn't until I was caged up like a rabid dog in some filthy cell, stripped of everything, and desperate for change, that I *heard the still, small voice* of Jesus, my Creator, and *responded* to Him.

You see, even though we do not know each other, our stories are very much the same. Our creator God chose us before the foundation of the world as His special children. We were loved by Him before our parents ever met. We were in His heart to be born at a certain time, with certain gifts and talents created in us, to be used for His purpose. These gifts and talents were to bring us a sense of fulfillment and purpose as we learn to develop them serving others.

Let's refer to the Bible to remind ourselves of this truth. On the lines provided after the scripture verse, please write it out three times:

Ephesians 2:10: For we are His workmanship, created in Christ Jesus, for good works, which God prepared beforehand that we should walk in them.

_____

_____

_____

_____

_____

_____

There are five important things Ephesians 2:10 tells us. Let's review them and write them out on the lines following.

Make them personal by inserting *I am* instead of *We*:

1. We are (I am) His workmanship.
2. We are (I am) created in Christ Jesus.
3. We are (I am) created for good works.
4. God prepared these good works beforehand for me.
5. We (I) should walk in these good works.

_____

_____

_____

_____

My first step back to God was to believe He exists, and that He created me for a life filled with *meaning* and *purpose*. I realized I was trying to fill an emptiness deep inside with things that were not only *not fulfilling*, but they were actually *stealing my life from me*. If something didn't change, I would certainly end up in the depths of hell, in this life, and the life to come.

In my darkest hour, when I was caged up, Jesus came to *rescue* me. He sent someone into prison to me. This person annoyed me to no end, but eventually this caring, committed servant of God got through to me.

In my darkest hour, when I was caged up, Jesus came to rescue me.

One day, He came to my cell because I was in lock down and said, "Hudson, what are you running from? Why are you so hard-hearted? Don't you realize the potential you have to make something great out of your life? You don't have to keep this up, Hudson. You really don't. Give your life to Jesus. He created you for so much more than this. I'm praying for you, Hudson...I'm praying for you..."

Then he turned and walked away.

I watched that man walk until I couldn't see him anymore. I made my way to the back of my cell where a makeshift mirror hung above a bolted-down stainless steel desk. The mirror wasn't glass for obvious reasons, but I could make out my face. I stood there for the longest time, staring into the empty eyes of a complete stranger...his words penetrating my soul...

You don't have to keep this up, Hudson. You really don't. Just come to Jesus. He created you for big things. He gave you talent...give it all to Him...give Him your life...Hudson... He can make something good out of it...I'm praying for you, Alex...

I wish I could tell you that I dropped to my knees that very moment and gave my life to Jesus, but it would be years, and several more periods of prison time before that happened.

To this day, I have no idea who that man was. But he planted *the seed of hope* in my soul that would be watered for the next few years by others, until it sprouted into a life-giving plant.

So, I'm coming to you, just like that man came to me. Write your name in the blanks and then read it out loud to yourself.

_____, *what are you running from? Why are you so hard-hearted? Don't you realize the potential you have to make something great out of your life? You don't have to keep this up,* _____. *You really don't. Give your life to Jesus. He created you for so much more than this. I'm praying for you,* _____. *I'm praying for you.*

Will you answer God's call for your life today? Will you do what I *finally* did before it is too late? Will you admit you are at the end of your rope, and there is no hope outside of giving your life over to God?

Are you tired of the life you have been living? Are you ready to make the choice to receive Jesus into your life, and allow Him to take control?

If you are, pray this prayer with me…

Jesus, I come to You as humbly as I know how, realizing my life is out of control, and I cannot do anything to save myself. I believe You are the Son of God, and came to this world in human flesh to die for my sins. I believe You died on the cross, You were buried, and rose from the dead on the third day. I believe You are seated at the right hand of God our Father, making intercession for me. I ask You to come into my life, and make Your home in my heart. I ask You to teach me, guide me, and help me to live my life pleasing to You. Please accept me into Your heavenly family, and help me become the person You created me to be. Help me to recognize the gifts and talents You created in me. Help me to spread Your life-giving Word to those who still don't know You. Thank You for accepting me into Your family, and freeing me from my sin. Amen.

Read and write the following verses out from the *Life Recovery Bible*. I encourage you to memorize them!

John 1:12-13 But to all who believed him and accepted him, he gave the right to become children of God. They are reborn-not with a physical birth resulting from human passion or plan, but a birth that comes from God.

_____

_____

_____

_____

You are NOW a child of God!
Your life can and will change!
You are no longer destructive-driven by the devil!
You are destiny-driven by the Spirit of God!

Fill in your name:

I, _____ am now a child of God!
I, _____ can and will change!
I, _____ am no longer destructive-driven by the devil!
I, _____ am destiny-driven by the Spirit of God!

Before we move on, I would like to give you an opportunity to *thank Jesus* for what He has done, is doing, and is about to do in your life!!!

_____
_____
_____
_____
_____
_____
_____
_____
_____
_____
_____
_____

Chapter 3

Tragedy's Triumph

Now that you have come to Jesus, and are a *child of God*, you can resume our study with *hope* and *anticipation* of a *promising future*. You are *no longer bound* to a life filled with darkness. You are *no longer bound* to the lies of the devil and his plans for your life…

You have been set free!!! Jesus has set you free!!!

Jesus lives inside of you, and you are His. You are now a child of the Most High God, and He will reveal His plans for your life as you learn to walk with Him day by day.

Please read Isaiah 61:1-3 with me. This passage is talking about Jesus:

The Spirit of the Lord God is upon Me, because the Lord has anointed Me to preach good tidings to the poor; He has sent Me to heal the brokenhearted, to proclaim liberty to the captives, and the opening of the prison to those who are bound; To proclaim the acceptable year of the Lord, And the day of vengeance of our God; To comfort all who mourn, To console those who mourn in Zion, To give them beauty for ashes, The oil of joy for mourning, The garment of praise for the spirit of heaviness; That they may be called trees of righteousness, The planting of the Lord, that He may be glorified.

List the things God sent Jesus to do:

1. He anointed Him to _____ to the poor.
2. He sent Him to_____ the brokenhearted.
3. He sent Him to_____ to the captives.
4. He sent Him to_____ to those who are bound.
5. He sent Him to_____ all who mourn.
6. He sent Him to give them _____ for ashes.
7. He sent Him to give _____ for mourning.

No matter where you are in life, God has a plan to take every dark, evil thing that has happened, and turn it into something good. God sent Jesus to do for you what you could not do for yourself...

SET YOU FREE TO BE WHO YOU WERE CREATED TO BE!!!

It took me *years* to realize what you have just come to realize...**Jesus came to set me free, not to inhibit me.** Why it took me so long, I can't tell you. But, I do know one thing...once I realized what was going on, I wanted everyone to know!

Of course, I went to the one person I thought would listen...Hillbilly. I want to share our story with you so you can see what God can do in the midst of deep darkness. And, how, if you will let Him, He can bring you out of your despair, and make something beautiful out of your life.

Because we lack understanding of just how important we are to God, we go through life searching for love and acceptance in all kinds of crazy places, only to come up empty in the end. We find ourselves stuck in an endless, disappointing search, looking for meaning and purpose. Desperate for change, we run here and there, trying all sorts of things to fill the emptiness that threatens to destroy us.

Hopefully our story will encourage *you to choose* the path that leads to life, not death. When tragedy struck, Hillbilly and I both had choices to make...which way will we go? What path will we follow? Will we allow circumstances and people to dictate the course of our lives? Will we hear God's call and follow Him?

Hillbilly and me…we go back a long way. We've done everything there is to do to try to fill our empty lives, and heal our deep wounds. Nothing worked, and prison was added to the equation. So, we ended up empty, wounded, *and in prison.*

My prison was a jury-decided *incarceration* with buildings and barbed wire; his was a self-induced *isolation* in a damp, dark barn. They were two *different types* of prisons, *but prisons nonetheless.*

The crazy thing about our story is that ***it didn't start out*** that way…

Hillbilly's barn wasn't always the flop house it is now. It wasn't always a dark, depressing hangout, reeking of death. It was a safe place where kids could come after school to sketch, play guitar, paint, write, learn crafts, and learn how to run a business. It was *full of life* and *hope* for a *better future.*

Tragedy and intense grief hit Hillbilly's family during his first year of college.

Hillbilly's parents owned *Harvest Acres*, a large farm that provided produce and dairy products for the surrounding community. It was a very successful business, and Hillbilly went to college to learn all he could about business so he could continue running the farm after his parents passed on.

Tragedy and intense grief hit Hillbilly's family during his first year of college. He was away at school when he got the call. His kid brother, Derek, was hanging with some guys on the corner of E. Main and Liberty when things got out of hand. Fists started flying, and, out of nowhere, a switchblade sliced Derek in the neck. Everyone split…they left him bleeding and crawling after them until he collapsed.

After Derek's funeral, Hillbilly took a leave of absence from college, and started a club at the farm for kids so they'd have a place to go instead of hanging out on the street after school. He called it *Triple H…**Harvest Happy Hour…THE** place to be after school*…in honor of his kid brother, Derek…Hillbilly's personal tragedy from the streets.

Triple H was a huge success. Kids from all over came to *Harvest Acres* after school to hang out. Activity school buses brought them, and the barn was buzzing with artists of all kinds. Kids who did not have artistic ability or interest in creativity were trained in planting, harvesting, milking, cheese making, and business planning. Several kids in my class went on to start their own businesses, and became successful members of society using the things they learned at *Triple H*. Unfortunately, due to my inability to make good choices, I was not one of them...

Anyhow, in comes Alex Hudson...yes, one of the activity bus students...not by *my choice*, but by detention! One of the more *difficult* students in my class, my detention teacher thought *Triple H* at Harvest Acres would help straighten me out!

And, for a time it did. Hillbilly made it clear to me the first day I arrived and tried to pull some of my crap, that he was in charge, and what it would cost me if I didn't abide by his rules. This was *his place, his program, his rules, and his authority*. I learned real fast that I wouldn't be able to pull anything over on him because he was as sly as me. This caused me to *respect* him...and, at that time, *I didn't respect anybody.*

A mutual respect between the two of us grew, and was the foundation for a friendship that would take us...to the deep dark places of our separate prisons.

I started *looking forward* to going to *Triple H* after school and it *really* did me some good. I was a better student during school because I didn't want to screw up being able to go. I learned everything Hillbilly knew about farming, and actually got to enjoy it. It wasn't very long until I moved up in the ranks, and became his right hand man. A mutual respect between the two of us grew, and was the foundation for a friendship that would take us from the mountain top of *Triple H* at *Harvest Acres* to the deep dark places of our separate prisons.

Hillbilly's parents retired to the mountains and sold him the farm. He continued running *Triple H* until the day he met Sarah Jane. Well, he didn't completely stop, like all of a sudden, but his loyalty was definitely being split between Sarah Jane and *Triple H*. Sarah Jane received about 99% of his attention!

Sarah Jane had a hold on him, and he didn't seem to mind. He spent less and less time at *Triple H* with me and the kids, and informed me one day that *Triple H* was my baby now, and that he had promoted me to Senior Executive.

Hillbilly isolated himself with his new love, and eventually I only saw him once every other week or so. Sarah Jane became his whole world. It was as though they were one body, soul, and mind. It was kind of creepy, but I tried to be happy for them.

One day Hillbilly came barging in to *Triple H* with Sarah Jane clinging to his side. He had the biggest smile I'd ever seen. He had a megaphone in his hand, the kind you see on the old movies that political candidates used in town squares to shout out to the people.

They had the same clothes on…sort of…the same colors at least, and he was shouting out on and on about a baby…they were going to have a baby!!! They danced around in a circle, Hillbilly with the megaphone, and Sarah Jane glued to his side. They looked like a top spinning around in a circus. The kids stopped writing, sketching, or whatever they were doing, and just stared at them.

D---, I thought. Wonder how this is all going to go down? I'll NEVER see him now. First, Sarah Jane, and now a little…? Well, Hudson, get some respect together and go shake the happy man's hand and hug the little mamma-to-be…

Fireside Chat
Tragedy's Triumph

No matter what is going on in our lives, we can be sure the gifts and talents God created in us when He gave us life will remain. Even in the midst of tragedy, God can produce something good.

Let's re-read our foundational verse and write it out:

Ephesians 2:10 For we are His workmanship, created in Christ Jesus, for good works, which God prepared beforehand that we should walk in them.

_____

_____

_____

God has created each of us with gifts, talents, resources, and desires, to make a difference in this world. We are not here simply to take up time and space. No matter where we are, or what we have done, these gifts and talents can be used by Him to make positive, long lasting changes in the lives of those around us.

Let's read what the Bible has to say in Romans 11:28-29 from The Life Recovery Bible. Write it out on the lines following...

Many of the people of Israel are now enemies of the Good News, and this benefits you Gentiles. Yet they are still the people he loves because he chose their ancestors Abraham, Isaac, and Jacob. For God's gifts and his call can never be withdrawn.

_____

_____

_____

_____

_____

Let's write out Romans 11: 29…

For God's gifts and his call can never be withdrawn.

God created the People of Israel to make His love and understanding known all over the world, but they became enemies of this Good News. God did not give up on them because He loved them. The Bible tells us that their gifts and callings can never be withdrawn.

This is great news for us! God is no respecter of persons. In other words, He does not show favorites, or remove gifts or callings from anyone.

THIS INCLUDES YOU!!!

Let's read more about this in Romans 12:3-21 from The Life Recovery Bible…

Because of the privilege and authority God has given me, I give each of you this warning: Don't think you are better than you really are. Be honest in your evaluation of yourselves, measuring yourselves, by the faith God has given us. Just as our bodies have many parts and each part has a special function, so it is with Christ's body. We are many parts of one body, and we all belong to each other.

In His grace, God has given us different gifts for doing certain things well. So if God has given you the ability to prophesy, speak out with as much faith as God has given you. If your gift is serving others, serve them well. If you are a teacher, teach well. If your gift is to encourage others, be encouraging. If it is giving, give generously. If God has given you leadership ability, take the responsibility seriously. And if you have a gift for showing kindness to others, do it gladly.

Don't just pretend to love others. Really love them. Hate what is wrong. Hold tightly to what is good. Love each other with genuine affection and take delight in honoring each other. Never be lazy, but work hard and serve the Lord enthusiastically. Rejoice in our confident hope. Be patient in trouble, and keep on praying. When God's people are in need, be ready to help them. Always be eager to practice hospitality.

Bless those who persecute you. Don't curse them; pray that God will bless them. Be happy with those who are happy, and weep with those who weep. Live in harmony with each other. Don't be too proud to enjoy the company of ordinary people. And don't think you know it all!

Never pay back evil with more evil. Do things in such a way that everyone can see you are honorable. Do all that you can to live in peace with everyone.

Dear friends, never take revenge. Leave that to the righteous anger of God. For the Scriptures say, "I will take revenge; I will pay them back," says the Lord. Instead," If your enemies are hungry, feed them. If they are thirsty, give them something to drink. In doing this, you will heap burning coals of shame on their heads." Don't let evil conquer you, but conquer evil by doing good.

As we learned earlier, we were not created simply to take up time and space, hoping to make it another day. We have learned that the gifts and talents God created in us cannot be removed...they are ever-present.

Our gifts and talents are still within us waiting to come out and be used by God to strengthen, encourage, and help others. No matter what we have done.

Read Romans 12:3-21 again. Ask God to show you what your gifts and talents are. On the following lines, write what you believe God is showing you. Gifts and talents are not limited to what is in this passage, but the way to use every gift is clearly stated. We are to strengthen, encourage, and help others.

Think about what you enjoy. Think about what type of people stir your heart when you see them in pain. These are good indicators of the gifts and talents God has created *in you* to help make positive changes in the lives of those *around you*.

_____

_____

_____

_____

_____

_____

_____

_____

_____

_____

Answer the following questions with our foundational verse in mind:

Ephesians 2:10 For we are His workmanship, created in Christ Jesus, for good works, which God prepared beforehand that we should walk in them.

What was the *personal tragedy* that caused Hillbilly to try to make a difference in his world?

_____

_____

_____

_____

What *personal tragedy* in *your life* could cause *you* to try to make a difference?

_____

_____

_____

How did Hillbilly respond to the *personal tragedy* in his life?

_____

_____

_____

Write about a *personal tragedy* in your life and how you can *positively respond* to it right now.

_____

_____

_____

_____

_____

What resources did Hillbilly have that he used to make a difference in the lives of those around him?

_____

_____

_____

_____

_____

What do you have (resources) where you are that you could use to make a difference in the lives of those around you?

_____

_____

_____

What was the outcome of Hillbilly's *positive response* to his *personal tragedy*?

_____

_____

What could be the outcome of a *positive response* to the tragedy in *your life* that *you* just wrote about?

_____

_____

Hillbilly used his *personal tragedy* as a source of determination to make a *positive impact in his community*. He had the resources of land and buildings, and the gift of leadership to make *Triple H* a success. He had a love for kids, and a desire to spare anyone else the grief his family experienced.

> *Hillbilly's personal tragedy was used by God to prevent more tragedies. His work with Triple H took the ashes of his life and turned them into something beautiful.*

Read the following verses (out loud if you can). They are talking about Jesus and what God **anointed** Him to do. What gifts and talents did God give Jesus in order to make a positive difference in the lives of those around Him?

As we read these verses, we come to realize Jesus has come *to help us walk through our personal tragedies*, and turn them into something that can be used to bring positive change in the lives of those around us...for generations to come.

Isaiah 61:1-4: "The Spirit of the Lord God is upon Me, Because the Lord has anointed Me to preach good tidings to the poor. He has sent Me to heal the brokenhearted, to proclaim liberty to the captives, and the opening of the prison to those who are bound. To proclaim the acceptable year of the Lord, and the day of vengeance of our God; To comfort all who mourn, To console those who mourn in Zion, To give them beauty for ashes, The oil of joy for mourning, The

garment of praise for the spirit of heaviness; That they may be called trees of righteousness, The planting of the Lord, that He may be glorified." And they shall rebuild the old ruins. They shall raise up the former desolations. And they shall repair the ruined cities, the desolations of many generations.

Re-read Isaiah 61:1-4 and answer the following questions…

What are the things Jesus was anointed (gifted and called) to do?

_____

_____

_____

_____

_____

Jesus was called to heal the brokenhearted, set the captive free, bring joy to those who were hurting, and tell people about God.

Why was Jesus anointed (gifted and called) to do the above things?

_____

_____

_____

_____

_____

Jesus was anointed (gifted and called) to raise people out of despair so they could help others, and ultimately show God's glory in the midst of trouble.

That's great…you might think…but what's it got to do with me?

Let's read John 20:19-22 from the Life Recovery Bible:

That Sunday evening the disciples were meeting behind locked doors because they were afraid of the Jewish leaders. Suddenly, Jesus was standing there among them! "Peace be with you," he said. As he spoke, he showed them the wounds in his hands and in his side. They were filled with joy when they saw the Lord! Again he said, "Peace be with you. As the Father has sent me, so I am sending you." Then he breathed on them and said, "Receive the Holy Spirit…"

Please write out John 20:21...

Again he said, "Peace be with you. As the Father has sent me, so I am sending you."

_____

_____

_____

_____

_____

Let's read John 20:19-22 again...from the Life Recovery Bible:

That Sunday evening the disciples were meeting behind locked doors because they were afraid of the Jewish leaders. Suddenly, Jesus was standing there among them! "Peace be with you," he said. As he spoke, he showed them the wounds in his hands and his side. They were filled with joy when they saw the Lord! Again he said, "Peace be with you. As the Father has sent me, so I am sending you." Then he breathed on them and said, "Receive the Holy Spirit..."

Several incredible things happened in these four short verses.

1. In the midst of pain and fear Jesus shows up!
2. He speaks peace to those around Him.
3. He shows the fearful His wounds, and they recognize Him.
4. When they realize Jesus is in the midst of their pain and fear, they are filled with joy.
5. Jesus speaks peace a second time to those in pain and fear, because He is about to send them on a mission.
6. Jesus speaks destiny and anointing over those who, just minutes ago, were in pain and fear.
7. Jesus commissions them, and tells them He is sending them out into the world, to do the same things the Father sent Him to do.
8. Jesus breathes on them, and they receive the Holy Spirit, who would enable them to do what He called them to do.

Let's take John 20:19-22 and make it personal. The disciples were behind locked doors because they were afraid. They were fearful. They were traumatized. Jesus had just been murdered, and they were afraid of the authorities.

Write about a time in your life when tragedy struck and you were afraid...

_____
_____
_____
_____
_____
_____

In the midst of their pain and fear, Jesus shows up and reveals Himself to the disciples. Write a prayer to Jesus, asking Him to show you where He was in the middle of your pain and fear. Then write what you believe He shows you.

_____
_____
_____
_____
_____
_____
_____
_____
_____
_____
_____
_____
_____
_____
_____
_____
_____
_____
_____

In the middle of the disciple's pain and fear, Jesus reveals Himself to them through _His own wounds_. He _identifies_ with their suffering, and _suffers with them_.

Isaiah 53:3-9 in the Life Recovery Bible tells us about _His wounds_...

He was despised and rejected-a man of sorrows, acquainted with deepest grief. We turned our backs on him and looked the other way. He was despised, and we did not care. Yet it was our weaknesses he carried; it was our sorrows that

weighed him down. And we thought his troubles were a punishment from God, a punishment for his own sins! But he was pierced for our rebellion, crushed for our sins. He was beaten so we could be whole. He was whipped so we could be healed.

All of us, like sheep, have strayed away. We have left God's paths to follow our own. Yet the Lord laid on him the sins of us all.

He was oppressed and treated harshly, yet he never said a word. He was led like a lamb to the slaughter. And as a sheep is silent before the shearers, he did not open his mouth. Unjustly condemned, he was led away. No one cared that he died without descendants, that his life was cut short in midstream.

But he was struck down for the rebellion of my people. He had done no wrong and had never deceived anyone. But he was buried like a criminal; he was put in a rich man's grave.

Jesus' wounds were deep. His closest friends deserted Him. His own creation mocked Him, spit on Him, brutally beat Him, stripped Him, and nailed Him to a tree. He understands the pain of rejection, fear, uncertainty, and abandonment. He can be trusted to take your most painful situations, and truly care.

In the midst of the disciple's pain and fear, Jesus stands with them. But, He does not reveal Himself to them to simply suffer with them. He wants to take them from their suffering and fear, and commission them out into the world to make a difference. He wants to turn their ashes into beauty.

On the following lines, write a prayer to Jesus, asking Him to help you make beauty out of the ashes in your life. Be specific. Talk to Him as you would your most trusted friend.

Dear Jesus,

_____

_____

_____

_____

_____

_____

_____

_____

_____

_____

_____

_____

_____

_____

_____

_____

_____

_____

We can be sure that if we call on Jesus in our darkest hour, He will come to us with understanding and love. He will stand with us, and walk with us through the pain and fear. He will encourage us to use what we have learned in our darkest hour to help someone else.

Now…back to our story…

Ephesians 4:29, - 5:29 - Mouth - body
Matthew 16:19   Power - Strongholds
Luke 10:19   Power - Strongholds

Ephesians 4:29, 5:39 - Mouth - body

Matthew 26:19 Power = Strongholds

Luke 16:19   Power + Strongholds

Chapter 4

Isolation's Inside Job

Things were going along pretty good at *Triple H*, as well as can be expected when you're dealing with a bunch of co-ed, hormonally imbalanced teens. Every once in a while we'd have to call the law if they wouldn't stop fighting, or sneaking around back to do whatever is was they shouldn't be doing. But, for the most part, *Triple H* was making a positive impact in the kid's lives, and keeping them off the streets.

That all came to a halt one day when Hillbilly staggered into the barn looking like he hadn't seen a shower in years. His hair was matted and plastered to his head. He hadn't shaved, it looked like, in weeks. His clothes were filthy, and he just plain STUNK! He was waving his fists, shouting incoherently at the top of his lungs, and tripping over anything that was in his way.

I hadn't seen him in a while, but I figured he was busy with the new baby. He called me the night before Sarah Jane was due to deliver, but I hadn't heard from him since. I didn't really think much about it because of how they were...all stuck to themselves, and all...besides, I was busy running *Triple H*.

Anyhow, the kids looked at me for some kind of explanation, which, of course I had none. I stood there for a minute watching his bizarre behavior before it registered to me...*Hillbilly was down-right plastered!!!*

I didn't know what to do. This was against everything he believed in and taught!!! It was *the* number one thing that could get a kid thrown out of *Triple H*. I was so shocked I had to shake my head. It took me a minute to think of a plan of action.

He might have been older than me, but I needed to be the adult right then. I shouted, "Hillbilly, get into my office...*RIGHT NOW!*"

I grabbed him, dragged him over to my office, threw him into the room, and slammed the door shut. It was like dragging a lifeless, life-sized Raggedy Anne doll that weighed a ton. He went on and on about little Samuel and Sarah Jane until his anger turned into sobs. I couldn't understand him, but talking to him would have to wait. I needed to get back to the kids, and try to divert their attention.

I called my buddy Antonio Carlucci to see if he'd come by and give me a hand. I needed to get into that office and talk to Hillbilly, but I couldn't chance leaving all those kids without adult supervision.

He came to my rescue by whipping up several giant sized pizzas from his old man's pizza joint, and bringing them over. Everyone *loved* Carlucci's. It was *the place* to be during any television broadcasted sports event. The Carlucci family came over from Italy just a few generations ago, and settled in our small community to keep from getting swallowed up in the big city, like most of their relatives did.

Mrs. Carlucci stayed at home keeping house while Mr. Carlucci and the boys ran the pizza joint. I often wondered how they were able to afford the stuff they had, but I never asked any questions. It was just a matter of time after Hillbilly staggered into the barn that day that I would find out, and begin my downward spiral into darkness.

Carlucci entertained the kids with pizza, sodas, and a game of volleyball out in the back field while I tried to make some sense out of what was going on with Hillbilly. I spent over an hour with him, and got virtually nowhere. He staggered, yelled, threw a few things, and finally ended up on the floor, sobbing. Our non-productive *discussion* was interrupted by the rumble of almost twenty teenagers running and shouting at each other. I told Hillbilly to stay put while I went out to see what was happening.

I was stunned. Carlucci was nowhere in sight, and the kids were running wild all over the place. "Where's Mr. Carlucci?" I had to shout.

"Don't know." Ben, the group's spokesman, shouted back. "Some old guy came up from the other side of the field, and handed him something. Mr. Carlucci gave him some money, but did it sneaky-like, figuring we wouldn't see. Then he told us they were going to walk out to the road to meet somebody, and he never came back."

Man...I thought. What next? I've got Hillbilly falling to pieces in my office, Carlucci's cut out on me, and I've got to think of something fast.

I didn't have the energy or the wisdom to tackle this crisis, so I made an executive decision to call it a day.

"Ok kids...let's have a quick *Triple H* meeting, then it'll be time to clear out." We gathered together under the big maple tree, where we always meet when there's a crisis...like fights breaking out and that sort of thing. It's where we examine the situation as a group, and move on from there.

I didn't have the energy or the wisdom to tackle this crisis, so I made an *executive decision* to call it a day. "Awe! But Mr. Hudson..." It was clear they wanted to hang out longer, but I stood my ground. I couldn't take care of them and Hillbilly at the same time.

Moaning and groaning about the unfairness of it all, they headed toward the activity bus. One by one, they filed in. They plopped into their seats, folded their arms across their chests, and stared out the windows with pitiful looks of disappointment as the bus pulled away. I watched them until they disappeared around the corner. I had no idea as I headed back to my office to deal with Hillbilly, that they would be the last bunch of kids to ever leave *Triple H*.

Two invisible dark clouds hovered over Harvest Acres that threatened to steal all of our destinies. One was boredom, the other tragedy. Hillbilly and I were about to begin a lifestyle that would be against everything *Triple H* stood for...

* * *

Sleet pelted our foreheads as I stood with Hillbilly a few days later watching Sarah Jane and Samuel being lowered into the ground. I never did find out exactly what happened...He wouldn't talk about it...

What he did say was, "Hudson...you know... it just ain't right that a man should have to put his son in a shoe box, and bury him in the backyard beside his Mamma, then, look down at both their graves all at the same time. It just ain't right, Hudson....don't want nobody to mention it ever again...ya hear?"

"Yeah...Hillbilly...I hear."

"Hudson?"

"Yeah...Hillbilly?"

"Help me cover my wife an' my boy?"

"Sure...Hillbilly...sure."

The sound shoveling makes when you're digging dirt to cover a grave is different than shoveling something for any other reason. It's plain sickening. I looked into those graves and thought, *how does a man survive something like this?*

Word around town was that Sarah Jane died from complications during delivery, and Samuel died a crib death.

Word around town was that Sarah Jane died from complications during delivery, and Samuel died a crib death. I don't put much stock in town chatter, and that's really irrelevant anyway, because, the whole thing, it just about killed Hillbilly too.

To say that Hillbilly changed overnight is an understatement. He marched away from Sarah Jane and Samuel's graves without a word. I started to follow him, but he held his hand up and said, "Hudson, where I'm headed is no good. I don't want you following me." And, with that, he disappeared over the hill heading toward the part of town the law won't even go. I knew it was useless to try to stop him, so I turned and walked away.

It would be several months before I ran into Hillbilly. I was hanging out in front of the courthouse, waiting to meet Carlucci, when he came out the front door.

"Hey Hillbilly," I shouted. "Wha'cha doing in there? Where you been?"

"Hey, Hudson! Got me a ticket for loitering down the hill the other day. Had to 'round up some cash and pay it off. Keeping to myself 'ceptin when the boys come up to the barn to work off a good hangover, and keep away from the law…did get me some companionship though."

"Well, Hillbilly, you don't waste no time, do you?!" I said. "What's her name?"

Hillbilly ignored my rude comment and said, "No *her* about it, Hudson. *His* name is Harrison."

"His name???"

"Yeah, Hudson…now don't go getting all riled up. Harrison's a horse…got him from an old friend who couldn't take care of him anymore. Named him after George…you know…George Harrison from the *Beatles*."

"Anyhow, he suits me just fine. He don't give me no lip. I don't have to watch him wondering what he's doing…keeps me company while I drink my hooch…it's just me, Harrison, my hooch, and that's all…cept'n when the boys come up. Got anything to say about that?" Hillbilly tipped an old ragged-looking hat toward me.

"No Hillbilly, not a thing."

"Me and Harrison, we're good for each other. He didn't have no home, and mine was empty. So, yeah we're good for each other. C'mon up sometime an' see fer yerself."

"Maybe sometime, Hillbilly, maybe sometime."

Nothing or no one could ever take the place of Sarah Jane and Samuel, but I suppose Harrison gave Hillbilly a reason to keep on living. He never stopped hitting the booze after they died, but taking care of Harrison kept him busy …then tragedy hit…*again.*

We had an extremely brutal winter the year Harrison died. It was relentless, not a day above zero for weeks at a time, or so it seemed. Harrison was old, and not in the best of health. Personally, I never thought he'd live as long as he did. I know a big part of Hillbilly died with Sarah Jane and Samuel, but now Harrison?

My phone rang about midnight. I checked caller ID and it was Hillbilly. *What's he want now?* He had this annoying habit of calling me in the middle of the night when he was plastered. I was tempted to ignore the call, but something told me to pick it up.

"Hudson..." His voice drifted and I could hardly hear him. I figured he was high or something, and I wasn't in the mood for his babble.

"Yeah...Hillbilly?"

"You got'a c'mon over here, Hudson, it's Harrison."

"Hillbilly, get some sleep. I'll be over in the morning."

"Hudson..."

"Later Hillbilly." I hung up.

Hillbilly was in the barn the next morning when I found him. He was sitting in the dark, wrapped up in Harrison's blanket. He looked horrible. I don't think he stopped drinking the whole night or got any sleep at all.

"Awe...Hudson..." He looked up at me with a blank stare.

"Hillbilly, what happened?" I reached down to help him up. Harrison's blanket slipped off his shoulders and onto the floor. I moved toward it...

"No, Hudson. Leave it be. Let's go into the house."

We sat in front of the kitchen window looking out over the snow-covered field.

"Hudson, you've known me long enough to know I eat my hangover breakfast in front of this here window so I can keep my eye on the field...just in case any low-life tries to sneak in behind the barn, and thieve me of my moonshine. You know it good as I'm sitting here telling you. Well, anyhow, you know my eyesight's been getting pretty bad, so at first I thought nothing of it."

"But then, listen up, Hudson. I thought I saw a big brown spot in the snow far out in the field. You know, where my property ends and the County Park starts? Didn't make no sense to me since we'd just got dumped on last night. I couldn't even open the front door this morning 'cause there was so much snow. Weather channel says we got 6-8inches of the stuff. So, I'm thinking…*what's that brown spot in the far field in the middle of all that snow?*"

> **Tears filled old Hillbilly's eyes. He pounded his fist on the table so hard I wondered why it or the table didn't break.**

"Then Hudson, just as I was thinking…*what's that brown spot out there in the far field??? It moved.* Yeah! Done plum freaked me out! I was filling up on the best hangover breakfast I've cooked myself in a long time…them hash browns sure was sloshing around my belly soaking up all the booze…I shook my head and saw it…the big brown spot…Hudson…it moved again…"

"Anyhow, Hudson…Listen to this…" Tears filled old Hillbilly's eyes. He pounded his fist on the table so hard I wondered why it *or* the table didn't break. "Hudson, there was only one explanation, and I just couldn't face it. You know… brown spots in the snow don't move unless it's something alive…getting ready to die."

He got up from the table and started pacing. "I couldn't stand it Hudson. I knew it was Harrison lying out there in the freezing cold. It *had* to be Harrison…I just knew it. He was lying in the snow with more of the crap falling on him…big, fat flakes they were…"

"I screamed…HARRISON!!! …and started feeling real sick like…you know…"

"I was in bad shape, Hudson because I was hung over to beat the band. My gut did a couple rollovers, and I headed for the john. I'm here to tell ya Hudson…all my breakfast, well let's just say, it wasn't pretty."

"I had it together enough to call the vet, but I got her answering service. They told me she was at another house call, and it might be a couple hours till she could get here to Harrison."

"I knew if I didn't get him up on his feet, he' be history. You know Hudson...I told you more than once...Harrison gave me *the only* reason not to check myself out'a this rotten life when Sarah Jane and Samuel passed. He loved me sober or drunk, in control or flipped out. Didn't matter to him, I was me and he was..."

Hillbilly slouched down on his old, worn out couch, and cupped his face in his hands. Uncontrollable sobs echoed through the room. I stood to comfort him, and he held his hand up.

"No, Hudson. I know what you're trying to do, and I'm grateful. But, really, Hudson, I want to be alone...the vet never made it. I went out to Harrison. He was still alive. I tried to help him get up but he was so heavy...he was so heavy, Hudson. He tried to get up but didn't have the strength. He tried and tried...it was awful watching him. I think he finally gave up. He just laid there looking at me with terror in his eyes."

"Hudson, he was so cold. I stood over him, I was crying. Yeah, me...big, bad Hillbilly, standing out in a field crying over a horse with snow falling on both of us. I watched them tears fall and freeze on his freezing body. He was *so* cold. I looked at him...straight in the eyes, Hudson. I know my horse. He was begging me not to let him lay there and freeze to death. Begging me, Hudson. His eyes was begging...*Hillbilly do it...please...don't let me lay here till I freeze to death...*"

"I went over to the barn and got his blanket. I laid it over his cold, cold body. He was barely breathing...short breaths, Hudson. His eyes were so tired-looking. So tired...Hudson...too tired to beg anymore."

"I knelt down beside his head so's he could hear me and said, "Harrison, you've been the best friend I could ever have. You've taken me places I never thought I'd go after Sara Jane and Samuel died. You took me to a happy place when I was so sad. You gave me a reason to live when I thought surely there wasn't. Harrison, only because I love you so much will I do the unthinkable. I'll do it for you...rest in peace my friend..."

"I reached down and stroked the side of his face. Hudson, he understood me, because the look in his eyes went from terror to peace. I put my cheek on his and memories of us riding together through the fields and woods flashed through my mind...beautiful memories..."

"I stood up, sobbing. Then I went to the shed and grabbed my shotgun."

Hillbilly slowly walked over to the back window, looked out over the field, and said, "Hudson, I had them bury him out there under the old elm tree where we used to stop on a hot day after a ride. I'd sit and sip me a cold one. Harrison got him a few carrots for a snack, ate them right out of my hand. And we'd just be there a spell before we'd come back in."

"That was *our place*…now he's out there, and I'm in here."

"And…I got two buried out there under the maple tree…my Sarah Jane and my boy, Samuel."

"No, Hudson…you go on now. I don't mean no disrespect or nothing, but I just want to be left alone. First Sarah Jane and my boy Samuel. Now Harrison. Don't want nobody coming over to old Hillbilly's no more. Me an' my hooch's all I need, and all I want. Now…you go on now an' leave old Hillbilly alone."

After Harrison died, he lost all will to live. He just lived in isolation and drank to forget.

He opened the front door, sipping his moonshine, and, I walked out.

Hillbilly's isolation got so bad that he had no idea what was going on out in the barn. People were coming in and out at all hours, dealing drugs, and stealing from him. He spent most of his time in his house, passed out on the floor. After Harrison died, he lost all will to live. He just lived in isolation and drank to forget.

One day he ventured out into the barn because a loud pop woke him up. "What the h---'s going on in here?" He shouted as he walked into what seemed like a fourth of July celebration…and it was the middle of April!

Men and women were lying all around on filthy mattresses, and he had no idea where they came from…the people or the mattresses. A gray cloud of sweet-smelling pot filled the air, and syringes were lying all over the place. He had to stumble over mounds of broken glass to get to the other side of the building to find out what was going on.

He said, "*WHAT THE H--- is going on here? Who __are__ you people?*" He picked up a whiskey bottle that somehow escaped a previous bottle battle, and smashed it against one of the poles. The sound of shattering glass caused some of his unwanted guests to notice him standing there. I was one of them.

"Hudson...what are *you, of all people* doing here? You crazy, man?"

"Hillbilly, don't you remember? Last week...in the back room of Carlucci's at the poker table...you paid up by telling him he could use the barn to crash at any time. I just came along for the ride...to see what's happening."

"I don't remember no such thing...Hudson."

He was hot, and packing something Hillbilly didn't want to be on the wrong side of.

Carlucci and a woman came out from behind a sheet that was hanging from the rafters. He was hot, and packing something Hillbilly didn't want to be on the wrong side of.

"Hey, hey, Carlucci. Yeah, you're right. I guess I just had me a *senior moment.* All y'all are welcome anytime." Hillbilly's bottle shook in his hands.

"Thought you'd see it my way..." Carlucci and his girl turned around and went back behind the sheet.

"Hillbilly, you don't want to mess with Carlucci...really you don't." I said.

"Yeah, Hudson, I know...I just hate to see you up in all this mess..."

"It's ok Hillbilly...Carlucci's got my back."

"STAND BACK!!! HANDS UP IN THE AIR!!! DON'T MOVE!!!" Blue-suited men and women ran in like a SWAT team and surrounded us. Screaming sirens threatened to split my eardrums. Flashing lights filled the entrance-way to the barn as cars were slammed into park, blocking the door. There was no way out.

Before I could think my next thought, my arms were pulled in directions they weren't created to be pulled in, and I heard a click as the cuffs clamped them together behind my back.

Sh-t! I thought…*where's Carlucci now?* Reality hit like a two-by-six on the back of my head. I heard squealing tires as his T-bird split the scene…so much for Carlucci having my back…eh? *Hudson, you fool.* I thought.

Carlucci's empty promises taunt me as they poured me into the squad car. One night after hanging with him and his thugs, he took me into the back room at the pizza joint and said, "You in, Hudson?"

"Yeah, Carlucci, I'm in."

I learned fast, was good, and *loyal.* He said he liked that about me…I was *loyal.* I became his right-hand man, just like I was Hillbilly's at Triple H…except, this right-hand man position came with some pretty heavy consequences. At first it was all good…fast cars…fast women…the best highs, and respect in town. Carlucci was sly, lying through his teeth. He said, "Stick with me kid, and you'll never get caught. I'll *always* have your back."

Yeah, Hudson, you fool. Once again Carlucci's split and left you hanging. One more free ride to the county jail…

Not only did Hillbilly's isolation mess with his God-given destiny, it messed with mine. This would be the first of many times I'd leave Hillbilly's barn in cuffs.

Take it from me and Hillbilly…isolation leads to no good thing…

Fireside Chat
Isolation's Inside Job

Isolation is another destiny thief. We are relational beings created to be in relationship with others and with God. We are the Body of Christ on the earth, and we cannot survive without each other.

Isolation lies to us and tells us we are better off without other people. It tells us we are protecting ourselves from being hurt or disappointed. It makes us believe we are self-sufficient. The longer we buy into these lies, the farther we get from the will of God.

Let's see what the Bible has to say about this in I Corinthians 12:12-27 from The Life Recovery Bible:

The human body has many parts, but the many parts make up one whole body. So it is with the body of Christ. Some of us are Jews, some are Gentiles, some are slaves, and some are free. But we have all been baptized into one body by one Spirit, and we all share the same Spirit.

Yes the body has many different parts, not just one part. If the foot says, "I am not a part of the body because I am not a hand," that does not make it any less a part of the body. And if the ear says, "I am not part of the body because I am not an eye," would that make it any less a part of the body? If the whole body were an eye, how would you hear? Or if your whole body were an ear, how would you smell anything?

But our bodies have many parts, and God has put each part just where he wants it. How strange a body would be if it had only one part! Yes, there are many parts, but only one body. The eye can never say to the hand, "I don't need you." The head can't say to the feet, "I don't need you."

In fact, some parts of the body that seem weakest and least important are actually the most necessary. And the parts we regard as less honorable are those we clothe with the greatest care. So we carefully protect those parts that should not be seen, while the more honorable parts do not require this special care. So God has put the body together such that extra honor and care are given to those parts that have less dignity. This makes for harmony among the members, so that all the members care for each other. If one part suffers, all the parts suffer with it, and if one part is honored, all the parts are glad. All of you together are Christ's body, and each of you is a part of it.

Write about a time when you just wanted to go into a closet and hide:

_____

_____

_____

_____

_____

_____

_____

_____

How did this isolation affect your life and the lives of those around you?

_____

_____

_____

_____

_____

_____

_____

Since I started telling you my story, we've run into three destiny-thieves. The first was boredom, the second, tragedy, and this most recent one…isolation. In every situation we face in our lives, we need to be aware of what is going on. The Bible tells us the devil comes to kill, to steal, and to destroy. His main goal is to stop us from entering our God-given destiny. (John 10:10) Look it up for yourself!

The devil used boredom, tragedy, isolation, and a combination of all three to steer Hillbilly and me off course.

On the following lines, write about a time when the same thing happened to you. Write about the outcome, how it has affected your life, and where you are now because of it. Use extra paper if you need to...

_____

_____

_____

_____

Jesus came to help us enter our destinies through Him. After my encounter with the Christian volunteer, God kept pursuing me until I finally submitted my life to Him. It is a win-win situation for us. We can live in harmony with God, ourselves, and others on this earth, with the promise of heaven after we leave here.

I am desperate for Hillbilly to find what I have found before it is too late. It's true that because I stuck by him when he was going through some pretty tough times, I ended up in places doing things I shouldn't have. And, those bad choices caused me to spend way too many years behind bars.

However, it is because I knew Hillbilly that I was introduced to my real destiny, that is to be an Aaron to a Moses. Let me explain...

Let's read Exodus 17: 8-13 together from The Life Recovery Bible:

While the people of Israel were still at Rephidim, the warriors of Amalek attacked them. Moses commanded Joshua, "Choose some men to go out and fight the army of Amalek for us. Tomorrow, I will stand at the top of the hill, holding the staff of God in my hand."

So Joshua did what Moses had commanded and fought the army of Amalek. Meanwhile, Moses, Aaron, and Hur climbed to the top of a nearby hill. As long as Moses held up the staff in his hand, the Israelites had the advantage. But whenever he dropped his hand, the Amalekites gained the advantage.

Moses' arms soon became so tired he could no longer hold them up. So Aaron and Hur found a stone for him to sit on. Then they stood on each side of Moses, holding up his hands. So his hands held steady until sunset. As a result, Joshua overwhelmed the army of Amalek in battle.

You see, friend, my God-given destiny was to be someone who supports another person who has the gift of leadership. I was operating in my God-given destiny every time I helped Hillbilly with *Triple H*, and even when I became Carlucci's right hand man.

Remember the Bible tells us our gifts and talents will never be withdrawn? So, guess what? They are going to be used one way or another...*either for good, or for evil.*

Can you see that my gift and talents were being used for both? When I was operating as Hillbilly's right hand man at *Triple H*, I was operating in my God-given destiny for good. When I was Carlucci's right hand man, I was still operating in my God-given destiny, but the gift was stolen by the devil to be used for evil.

Write the supporting verse out on the following lines to refresh your memory.

Romans 11:29 from The Life Recovery Bible:

For God's gifts and his call can never be withdrawn.

I want to challenge you before we move on to take an inventory of your life, and the choices you have made. Do you recognize any gifts and talents God has given you that you have used for good? Have those same gifts and talents been stolen from the enemy and used for evil?

In this next exercise, please write the gift or talent you believe God has given you, and place an X under the correct spot. Explain your answers...I'll go first so you know what I'm getting at. Come back to this exercise often. You are created with many gifts and talents!!! Use extra paper and be thorough.

GIFT/TALENT	USED FOR GOOD	USED FOR EVIL
Gift of Helps	X	X

Explanation: I used my gift of helps to assist both Hillbilly and Carlucci in their endeavors. Helping Hillbilly was positive, Carlucci negative. When I helped Hillbilly, we were helping others. When I helped Carlucci, we were breaking the law. The gift of helps is part of my God-given destiny that I need to use for Him.

_____

_____

_____

_____

_____

_____

_____

_____

_____

Celebrate the gifts and talents God Has given you! Make it a point to be on the lookout for the evil destiny—thieves that try to steer you off course. Don't let boredom, tragedy, or isolation stop you from being who you are created to be!!! Personal notes:

_____

_____

_____

_____

_____

_____

_____

_____

_____

_____

_____

_____

_____

_____

_____

_____

_____

_____

_____

_____

_____

Chapter 5

Evicting Excuses

I shake my head to bring myself back to reality. It is strange how an old, dilapidated, foul-smelling barn can take you back memory lane, to places better off forgotten…

I look around for any evidence of life…there is none. Hillbilly must have let Carlucci and his thugs have full reign. Surely these aren't the *same foul mattresses* that were here years ago?!? With all Carlucci's money, I can't believe he didn't do something with this place. I pull my knees up to my chin. It's *so cold* in here I'm not sure how much longer I can hang out.

Surely Sullivan's figured out I'm no threat, just a bored, jerk messing with his watchdog. I pray God will forgive my ignorance.

I change gears, and center my thoughts on my old friend. I heard he's still hanging out in his house, drinking day and night. He only comes out once in a while to make sure whoever's out here doesn't burn the place down.

Hillbilly's headed for destruction, not only in this life, but into the next, if he doesn't change something soon. His body's shriveled up from years of abusive isolation, and I believe his time is short.

Just as I am pondering his fate...Here he comes!!! *Thank You God! Maybe he'll listen to me today!!!*

My heart aches as I watch him stumble in. As soon as he spots me he slurs, "Hudson, what'cha doing here? This ain't open house, you know. My gut told me to get out here, someone might be layin' claim to some space that ain't their's. Carlucci know you're here?"

"Where you been, Hillbilly? Carlucci's sitting up in the courthouse waiting for his jury to be picked! He got busted for trafficking, and I'm not too sure they didn't snatch him up right here. Listen to me, friend! C'mon, put that thing down, just for a couple minutes!!!" I point to the bottle he's clutching. "You got'a get a grip on what's going on around here, and what's happening to you."

"Hudson, don't you go thinkin' you're gonn'a start preaching at me again...I mean it, Hudson. This is what I think of your crazy preaching..." He takes the top of his whiskey bottle and smashes it against the center pole.

"You gone plumb out of your mind! All your talk about getting saved!!! Saved from WHAT??? Born again...now that's crazier than the time you hit that crack and went sledding down the ski slopes at Christmas...said you was training for the Olympics toboggan."

"You are *crazy*! You gonn'a be BORN AGAIN when you's already BORN??? I think you done went behind my back and got my best bottle of moonshine or some of Carlucci's good snort, that's what I think!"

Hillbilly leans his back against the pole and slides down, landing in a puddle of booze and broken glass. "Now you done got me so worked up, I wasted a whole bottle of my best hooch." He wraps his hands around his head and starts moaning. "You got five minutes, man...five minutes. Then I'm off to my still...got some great hair-growing, gut-pleasin' stuff brewin' back there..."

"Hillbilly, *LISTEN TO ME.* I thought them people were crazy who came into *The County* preaching when I was locked up until *I LISTENED TO THEM.* C'mon Hillbilly...*LISTEN TO ME!*"

I sit down beside him and grab his right hand. "Go on...make the fist like we used to." I reach my right fist toward him. He grins, makes the fist, and we tap our knuckles together in the, *I got your back* pact, we made years ago.

"I'm telling you the truth Hillbilly, this is the most important *I got your back* knuckle pact I've ever made with you...beats the time the feds came snooping around the barn hunting you down. Remember that?"

He nods and grunts..."Hudson...I *hate* it when you corner me like this. Go ahead, you got five minutes, then I'm going to get me some more hooch. I'm way over due, look man, I got the shakes."

I grab his hand. "Hillbilly, this here info I'm about to tell you can change your life. You won't need that hooch, or any other stuff to keep the shakes away. Just look at me...you know how long it's been since I've hit *anything*? You know how long I been clean? Hillbilly, you can come clean too!"

"Never...Hudson...never. I'm too far gone... this ole boy'll never be clean...been a junkie long as I can remember, be a junkie long as I live, and die a junkie, Hudson. That's my lot in life...no better...no worse...Hillbilly the junkie...that's me."

> **"I'm telling you, Hillbilly, you are made for something great. You've just got to get your head out of the fog long enough to believe it for yourself."**

"Hillbilly... *NO!* That's what I'm trying to tell you...you don't have to keep living like this! You got potential, Hillbilly! I've seen it. I've watched you work with wood even when you're high. You are a skilled woodsman, Hillbilly. You could start your own business, and make enough money to live good, doing it the right way. I'm telling you, Hillbilly, you are made for something great. You've just got to get your head out of the fog long enough to believe it for yourself."

"No can do, Hudson...too old. Don't have the energy nor the wants to change now. Old Hillbilly...the junkie...yup that's who I am, and that's who I'll stay till my dyin' day...and don't give me any of that Jesus stuff, I'm not in the mood. Got'a get me some more hooch."

"Hillbilly...you said five minutes. You said you'd give me five minutes!"

"Ok suit yourself...I'm all ears." He leans his head back against the pole, and looks up toward the ceiling in attempt to show me how disinterested he is.

"Look here, Hillbilly. I pull out my pocket Bible. "You respect the Bible don't you?"

"Yeah, I suppose so. Grama Ella Mae used to rock beside my bed, and read it to me every night. Said it was God's Word and He couldn't lie. She'd rock in that old creakin' chair, and read till I'd be a snorin'. Liked that story about David and Goliath though...seems David had something going on that old Goliath didn't. Wonder how he pulled it off?" Hillbilly turns toward me with questioning eyes.

Whew! A rush of excitement hits me in the center of my gut...can't get any better than this. I've got an open door, and Hillbilly's going to lose track of time. God's got his attention and has prepared him to listen! All I got to do is open my mouth.

> **"Hillbilly...you want know what I think? You got a gift, man... you care about people... they call it the gift of compassion."**

"Hillbilly, what do you remember about David and Goliath?"

"Well, David was small, Goliath was huge, and David killed him dead with a slingshot. That's 'bout all. Cool story though. I always root for the underdog, you know...seems like I been one all my life...the underdog, I mean."

"Hillbilly...you want know what I think? You got a gift, man...you care about people...they call it the gift of compassion. It's just been twisted and used for all the wrong stuff. You give people a place to stay when they don't have one. You supply what they think they need when they don't have it. You share your space and your place with anyone who comes by. You *CARE*, Hillbilly, I know you do. No matter how blasted you get, *YOU STILL CARE*."

"You gave me a place to crash, and sort through some pretty crazy stuff, when my dad slammed into that tree, and my mamma split. Before Granny came to my rescue, you were there for me. You aren't a bad person, Hillbilly, just a bit off track. You got good qualities when you sober up. I'm telling you, Hillbilly, you can change and make something great out of the rest of your life. I'll never stop believing it man...never stop."

"Out of all the stories your Grandma read, you remember David and Goliath. Why? I think its cause God's trying to get your attention through that story. Hillbilly, you're just like David, you've been *fighting giants* all your life."

Hillbilly shifts and shakes his head. "I dunno Hudson. You's wastin' yer time with me... If'n I told you once, I told you a thousand times. I'll never change. Nobody'd want old Hillbilly for nothing but a crash pad and some good high. See, Hudson...Grama Ella Mae...she kept prayin' and prayin' and then one day she died. Since then ain't no more prayin' for old Hillbilly... so's he don't have a chance in h--- anymore."

"Hillbilly! That's a crock and you *KNOW* it! Don't cop out on me now, man. Your Grama's prayers had power then, and they have power now! Why do you think I'm still here trying to convince you that *you were created f*or so much more than this? It's your Grama's prayers. I'm telling you. And, you know the only reason *I'm* still alive, and not rotting in the big house is because of *my* Granny's prayers. If it can work for me, it can work for you. There's enough power floating around for both of us, enough for you to slay all the giants in your life...if you'd just *LISTEN*, Hillbilly, and tap into it."

"Look at what you're sitting in, man! Rot-gut booze and glass! You should be sitting at a workbench creating something incredible like *I KNOW* you can! But, no, here you are mumbling to me about running out of hooch, and being doomed to die as an old junkie without purpose or worth. It's a *CROCK*...Hillbilly...*A CROCK* and a *COPOUT*..."

He doesn't reply, and, for a minute, I hold my breath hoping I didn't screw up this incredible opportunity. Hillbilly isn't one to allow people to challenge him, and, if they try, he just plain throws them out.

I wait for him to make a move. He shifts again and picks up the broken bottle. He stares at it closely for a minute, then, slowly lays it on the floor between us. He runs his finger up and down its side and lifts his head. I freeze. I'm caught off guard by what I see.

His eyes are glazed over from the booze, but there is something else going on. I watch in stunned amazement as they slowly fill with water. He doesn't move as he stares at me. His brow rises, and he pleads with me. He wants to believe, but doesn't know how. *God is moving.* I'm sitting on Holy Ground with my friend, at a very critical time in his life, with a broken bottle of booze lying between us.

He starts humming and continues to run his fingers along the side of the broken bottle. "Hillbilly..." He raises his hand to stop me, and I notice blood trickling down his wrist. I reach out for him as he rolls himself into a ball, and continues to hum. I carefully inch closer through the broken glass, being careful not to cut myself.

"Hillbilly..." I try again.

"Hudson...Hudson...somethin's happnin' to me..." He's shaking. My eyes fill as I embrace my old friend; the one who introduced me to a life of false highs, women, and booze. "I'm here, old buddy," I say, as he rocks in my arms, sobbing, and humming that old familiar song...

Amazing grace, how sweet the sound, that saved a wretch like me...

He hums in perfect tune, and I join in, rocking with him. The sliver of light that was shining on my Bible earlier embraces us as we hum this sweet song of surrender together.

Hillbilly is broken, wounded, ready, and willing to listen...I can *feel* it. I can *truly* feel it. I'm sure the angels are singing, and heaven is rejoicing as Hillbilly rocks in God's love and forgiveness...

Our sweet, *holy ground* moment is interrupted as Hillbilly jerks and backs away from me, shouting profanity like I haven't heard since I was locked up. He staggers toward the front of the barn.

"My pa always told me, real men don't cry. He used to beat the living ---- out of me anytime I even showed the littlest hint of squawlin'. No...Hillbilly here...he don't cry! And, Hudson, if'n you let on to anybody that this here ever happened, I'll put a contract out on ya...you bet I will. My pa didn't raise no sissy...an' you an' yer Jesus talk ain't goin' turn me into one now!"

"Hillbilly!!!" I shout over his cursing, and grab him by the shoulder. He's staggering from the booze and whatever else he's on, but I'm able to hold him steady.

"Hillbilly, listen to me. Your pa was a good man. He wanted you to be able to make it in this world. He did what he thought was best. But, Hillbilly, on this thing, he was wrong."

"Hudson, I'm so messed up. You come in here, screwing with me...what you gone done that fer? Couldn't you jest leave old Hillbilly alone to die with his bottle of booze and crack? Why you come here bringin' up old memories and messin' with my already messed up head? Why...Hudson...why?"

With a heavy heart and water pouring out of my eyes, I watch as Hillbilly staggers out toward the shack he calls home.

"Because I *care* about you and what happens to you. And, because *Jesus* cares."

"See, Hudson, there you go again...with that *Jesus stuff*. Where was He when Pa died? Where was He, Hudson, when little Ella got run over?

He picks the broken bottle up, and waves it in the air. "Where...Hudson...where? He don't care nothin' 'bout old Hillbilly...an' sure enough He wouldn't want no slobberin' junkie like me in His heaven. And, if'n God is God, He sure wouldn't want no sissy of a man around, blubbering with water runnin' out'a his eyes...If'n Pa didn't want a sissy of a son, sure enough God wouldn't want one neither..."

With a heavy heart and water pouring out of *my* eyes, I watch as Hillbilly staggers out toward the shack he calls home. He mumbles something and kicks the side of the barn, still waving his broken bottle.

"Dam it to ----, Hudson! You come back here messin' with me and stirring up all kinds of crap...you get on out'a my barn and take your Jesus with you...old Hillbilly don't have no time for none of it...you get on out'a here, Hudson. It's time for old Hillbilly's afternoon nap, and I don't want nobody here wilst I'm sawin' logs."

"Hillbilly...wait..."

"I mean it, Hudson. Git hoofin'. I don't wan'a see you 'round these parts lessin' you comin' here to share some hooch or powder with me...I got no time for you *or* 'ur religion..." He smashes the bottle against the barn and walks away. I stare at the back of his tattered coat as he heads for the shack. "OK, Hillbilly. You got it. I won't be around to bother you no more."

He doesn't turn around or respond.

I lay the old blanket down and slowly walk toward the door. I take one last look around the barn and shake my head. My old friend's stuck in a life that's killing him. He's skin and bones. His eyes are sunk in with a blank stare that never goes away. I hear the old screen door slam shut as he enters the shack that he calls home. It's my cue to move on. I've done all I can do here...the rest is up to God.

Fireside Chat
Evicting Excuses

I'm certain God is working on Hillbilly, and I will not give up praying for him. There is no one too far away from God that they cannot be saved. There is no one too stuck in a destructive life that He cannot deliver. Do not give up on yourself or anyone else. God is continuously calling every soul back home to Him.

Read the following verses and write them out on the lines provided:

Isaiah 50:2 ...Is My hand shortened at all that it cannot redeem? Or have I no power to deliver?

_____

_____

_____

_____

_____

Isaiah 59:1 Behold, the Lord's hand is not shortened, that it cannot save; nor His ear heavy, that it cannot hear.

_____

_____

_____

Write in your own words what these verses mean to you:

_____

_____

_____

_____

_____

_____

_____

Let's take these verses and make them personal:

My Lord's hand is not too short that it cannot redeem me. My Lord has power to deliver me.

_____

_____

_____

Behold, my Lord's hand is not shortened, that it cannot save me, nor is His ear heavy, that He cannot hear me.

_____

_____

Who do you relate to the most in this part of our story? Alex, who is trying to help his friend come to Jesus? Or, Hillbilly, who wants to come to God, but is struggling? Explain your answer on the following lines:

_____

_____

_____

_____

_____

How do you think Alex is feeling as he walks away from Hillbilly? How would you feel?

_____

_____

_____

What do you think caused Hillbilly to throw Alex out?

_____

_____

_____

Excuses, excuses, excuses. At some point in time we are all full of excuses. We can't finish our homework because we don't feel good. We can't take out the garbage because it is too heavy. We can't brush our teeth because the toothpaste tastes horrible. We can't stop drinking, drugging, running around, because...because... because...

Jesus is well aware of our human nature to come up with excuses for anything, including His offer of salvation and deliverance.

Let's read it together…It is titled: *The parable of the Wedding Feast…*

Matthew 22:1-10: And Jesus answered and spoke to them again by parables and said: "The kingdom of heaven is like a certain king who arranged a marriage for his son, and sent out his servants to call those who were invited to the wedding; and they were not willing to come. Again, he sent out other servants, saying, 'Tell those who are invited, "See, I have prepared my dinner; my oxen and fatted cattle are killed, and all things are ready. Come to the wedding."' But they made light of it and went their ways, one to his own farm, another to his business. And the rest seized his servants, treated them spitefully, and killed them. But when the king heard about it, he was furious.

And he sent out his armies, destroyed those murderers, and burned up their city. Then he said to his servants, 'The wedding is ready, but those who were invited were not worthy. Therefore go into the highways, and as many as you find, invite to the wedding.' So those servants went out into the highways and gathered together all whom they found, both bad and good. And the wedding hall was filled with guests.

Re-read the *Parable of the Wedding Feast* and answer the following questions:

Who is the king?_____

Who are the servants? _____

What are people being invited to? _____

What were the people's excuses for not coming? _____

_____

What did some of the people do to the king's servants? _____

_____

Why do you think some of the people treated the king's servants badly and killed them? _____

When the king realized the people he invited didn't want to come, what did he do?

_____

_____

Do you see yourself in this story, and which part are you playing? _____

_____

_____

_____

_____

_____

Give an explanation of what you believe Jesus was trying to tell us through this story:

_____

_____

_____

_____

Now, match column A with column B:

__E__ king	A		invited from highways
_____ good servants	B		kingdom of heaven
_____ bad servants	C		those who tell others of the king
_____ wedding	D		invited from highways
__C__ prostitutes	E		Jesus
_____ prisoners	F		invited from highways
_____ alcoholics	G		servants who invite others
_____ poor	H		invited from highways
_____ hungry	I		those who kill the kings servants

Re-read Jesus' parable again and list the excuses the people gave the king for not accepting his offer:

_____

_____

_____

_____

Let's take a minute to discuss the king's offer. Jesus is explaining a spiritual truth by using a natural story so we can understand what He is trying to say. If we consider Jesus the king in our story, and the Kingdom of God the wedding, we will be able to understand some very important things concerning our lives, and our future.

This study we have been doing together has been about destiny and destiny-thieves. In *The Parable of the Wedding Feast*, Jesus shines the light on another destiny-thief... ***excuses and procrastination***.

In my encounter with Hillbilly, we see this destiny-thief in action. God is calling him, and I believe he *wants* to come, but his excuses are getting in the way.

Write down some of the excuses Hillbilly gives for not accepting Jesus' offer:

_____

_____

Now, let's get honest with ourselves. It is easy to read about Hillbilly and his struggles, but what about us? What about you? What are *your* excuses *right now* for not accepting Jesus' offer to you? Be specific. Be gut-level honest!

_____

_____

Let's re-read and re-write our verses from Isaiah:

Isaiah 50:2...Is my hand shortened at all that it cannot redeem? Or have I no power to deliver?

_____

_____

Isaiah 59:1... Behold, the Lord's hand is not shortened, that it cannot save; nor His ear heavy, that it cannot hear.

_____

_____

Let's pray over the excuses you wrote about using the verses in Isaiah...

Lord Jesus...I come to You with a willing heart, to repent of my excuses for not accepting Your offer of salvation and deliverance from the devil's work in my life. I repent of the excuse of _____ (pray this prayer for each excuse separately) and ask for Your help. My heart's desire is to follow You into the destiny You have for me. I renounce the devil and all he has to do with this excuse, and command him to leave me in Jesus' name. In its place, I receive Your will for my life and destiny. I receive Your still, small voice of guidance and renounce the voice of the devil. I declare that the devil has no authority in my life, because I am a blood-bought child of the Most High God. You bought and paid for me, and washed me in Your Blood as Revelation 1:5 declares. *I refuse to walk in the destiny the devil has planned for me, and declare that I will walk in Your truth, and the destiny You have planned for me.* Thank You, Lord Jesus, for revealing this excuse to me, and giving me the power to overcome its hold on my life. In Your powerful name. Amen.

Read and declare the following statement out loud over your life again:

I REFUSE TO WALK IN THE DESTINY THE DEVIL HAS PLANNED FOR ME, AND DECLARE THAT I WILL WALK IN GOD'S TRUTH, AND THE DESITNY HE HAS PLANNED FOR ME.

Chapter 6

Still, Small Voice

I leave Hillbilly's place with a heavy heart, wondering which way to head home. I figure I'd better stay away from old man Sullivan and his watchdog until things cool off. But something else is bugging me. This last encounter with Hillbilly has shaken me up. I'm doing some pretty serious soul-searching myself.

I look at my watch, surprised at how much time has passed since I left the court-house. Ms. Madeline's going to have my hide when I get home, and I don't blame her. She's not bad...actually...she's kept me out of the slammer more than once by her nagging and praying. I owe her a lot, and feel ashamed, the way I treat her sometimes.

I'm an adult now, and need to get it together. You'd think spending half my life locked up would change the way I look at things and treat life. But, no, God has to grab my attention with stuff like this encounter with Hillbilly when I get off track.

What am I doing? Where am I headed? Surely, my future holds more than barely surviving every day! The Bible says I am *more than a conqueror* and I'm teasing a watchdog and running from its owner for kicks??? How did I get to this point anyhow...*again?*

I avoid Mr. Sullivan and his watchdog by crossing town just south of his street which takes me through the woods behind our house. I notice a doe and her fawn running through the snow together. Clumps of white flakes shoot out behind them as they head toward the pond behind our house, searching for water...

As the deer pants for the water brooks so pants my soul for You, Oh God...Ps 42:1

I open the back door to the aroma of hot apple pie. Ms. Madeline bends down to reach inside the oven to retrieve her prize. Oh, how I love Ms. Madeline's hot apple pie! My thoughts of devouring a piece in front of the fire are interrupted...

Granny's warm smile greets me, and I feel a sense of great peace. Even though she's long gone, her wisdom lives on.

"Alex! Where have you been? It's almost dark! Why didn't you call me to come get you? You must be freezing...sit down and take off those boots! Go warm yourself by the fire...I do declare..."

Ms. Madeline keeps fussing around the kitchen, and I obey like a stray dog thankful for a warm place to call home. Go figure! I expected to be sabotaged with a million questions and endless nagging. I walk over to the fireplace and look at the pictures lining the mantel. Granny's warm smile greets me, and I feel a sense of great peace. Even though she's long gone, her wisdom lives on.

Alex...you're letting the devil back in little by little. He's just waiting for you to make one wrong move so he can own you again. Don't give him any more rope, Alex. He's itching to hang you, and stop you from becoming who God created you to be. Remember what we talked about so many times...the evil destiny- thieves?

Yeah, Granny, I do.

I smile at Granny's plump face, and sink down into her chair. She shed many, many tears, and prayed many, many prayers in this old chair. I rub my palms over the tops of the arms...*I know without a shadow of a doubt that I'm alive today because of the time she spent in this chair...* Although it is old, rickety, and worn, we consider it the foundation of this home, and we'll never replace it.

I stare into the fire, and let my mind wander to the scenes I just left at Hillbilly's. There are so many *destiny-thieves* in that place. There's the booze, drugs, sex, boredom, easy money, anger, disappointment, hopelessness, and fear. And, that's just what I saw in a few short hours…wonder how many more are ready to sink their teeth into Hillbilly and everyone else who hangs out there?

It all seems so hopeless. Hillbilly won't listen. He believes what he believes. I've got enough problems of my own to deal with right now. I don't need to waste my time caring about someone who obviously doesn't want anything to do with me or *my Jesus.*

Besides, I've got to get myself back together before I can even think about helping someone else. God's got to be pretty peeved at me by now. I can't seem to stick with Him even after all He's done for me. No wonder Hillbilly wouldn't listen. I'm just another loser, a Christian who can't stay a Christian. Nobody's going to ever take me seriously. Just look at me…one BIG loser.

Alex…the still, small voice…listen for the still, small voice…

It is Granny's voice coming back to rescue me. I know it so well. She had a way of straightening me out when I was all twisted up. She always used the Word of God to set me straight…said there's nothing like the Word.

One time I was locked up on a long stretch, and was about to go insane. I was losing all sense of reality, and suicide was coming to the forefront of my mind.

Granny sensed my despair in a letter and came to the rescue. It was not a long sermon filled with a bunch of do's and don'ts. It was full of love, concern, and Godly wisdom. It was *the* most simple, but powerful thing she ever taught me. She taught me to *listen for, and obey the still, small voice.*

Now, mind you, when you're locked up, it's probably not a good thing to admit you're hearing voices; especially if it gets out you're contemplating suicide. But, when Granny puts the Word of God in front of you and explains it, you just have to listen. You can't deny its power to change things.

So, there I was, teetering on the edge of insanity, and she writes and tells me to *listen for, and obey a still, small voice*! I didn't know whether to laugh or cry. I was in such a state of despair, I could hardly function. It was only a matter of time until the authorities would recognize my state of being, and, either put me in solitary, or send me to the shrinks.

Because Granny had been the only constant source of stability in my life, I chose to hear her out. Eventually I believed the Word of God for myself, and began to have a real relationship with Jesus through His *still, small voice.*

God had never left me; I just walked away from Him, and I was out of earshot.

It is precisely the *still, small voice* that caused me to do some serious soul-searching on the way home from Hillbilly's. God had never left me; I just walked away from Him, and I was out of *earshot.*

I'm thinking I need to get another dose of Granny's *still, small voice* letter. I put another log on the fire, and walk toward my room. I've kept every letter she's ever written me, and they are filed in boxes in my closet. I open the closet door, and I'm caught off guard by a box of old DVD's smacking me in the head.

Despite the cluttered condition of the closet, I have a meticulous filing system for Granny's letters. This one, I know, is in a box labeled, *Hearing God,* and I spot the box immediately. With a sense of peace, I retrieve the letter, and make my way back to Granny's chair.

My dear Alex,

I sense you are in a place now where you've never been before. I am sorry you're having such a hard time dealing with everything and everybody around you. Be sure your tears do not go unnoticed in the dark places. In Psalm 56:8-9 God tells us how important our tears and wilderness times are to Him. Here... just read it:

You number my wanderings; Put my tears into Your bottle; Are they not in Your book? When I cry out to You, Then my enemies will turn back; This I know because God is for me. Psalm 56:8-9

I am praying for you. There is nothing I can do from here, but let you know of my love, and continued prayers on your behalf. I can give you encouragement, compassion, and hope from my pen, but I cannot give you what you <u>really</u> need! You are looking in all the wrong places, Alex, for your satisfaction, identity, and worth.

There is only One Who can satisfy all your longings and desires. It's the Lord, Alex. He's the only One Who can rescue you. You must not despair, Alex. Your life is important, and you have a destiny in God. I don't know what it is, but He does. You must cry out to Him, Alex. That is when your enemies of fear, disappointment, discouragement, anger, bitterness, jealousy, and a host of other evil destiny-thieves will flee.

You cannot piggy-back on my relationship with Jesus. You cannot hang onto the coat tails of the preachers and teachers that come into your prison to minister. You have to have your own relationship with Jesus! You have been riding the fence, Alex. It is either all or nothing. It is not ok today and then you say, "Let's see what tomorrow brings."

You've got to decide who you will serve. Will you chose life over death? It is your choice, Alex. I cannot choose for you. Read God's challenge to you from Deuteronomy 30:19-20:

I call heaven and earth as witnesses today against you, that I have set before you life and death, blessing and cursing; therefore choose life, that both you and your descendants may live; that you may love the Lord your God, that you may obey His voice, and that you may cling to Him, for He is your life and the length of your days; and that you may dwell in the land which the Lord swore to your fathers, to Abraham, Isaac, and Jacob, to give them.

Choose life, today, Alex! Put behind you all the desires that call you into darkness. Choose the Lord today, Alex, and find your destiny. Choose the Lord and choose life!!!!

I want you to read a story in the Old Testament about a prophet named Elijah. Things weren't going his way, and he was running away. Then he got to the point where you are, Alex, he wanted to lie down and die. He even asked God to take his life!

*You are in a wilderness, Alex. The journey for you, like Elijah, is too hard for you. You must **arise** and eat and drink. You must eat from the Word of God for nourishment. You must drink from the word of God for cleansing. You will not survive if you don't eat and drink from the Word of God!*

Read the following verses and write them out to help you understand what I am saying…

But He answered and said, "It is written, 'Man shall not live by bread alone, but by every word that proceeds from the mouth of God.'" Matthew 4:4

_____

_____

**That He might sanctify and cleanse her with the washing of water by the word...
Ephesians 5:26**

_____

_____

_____

_____

I'm not sure if you even have a Bible anymore, so I'm going to write Elijah's story out here for you to read. I want you to pray before you read this. Get serious with God, and let Him know you are choosing life over death. You are no different than Elijah, Alex. You are on the run. You don't think your life is worth living. You are looking for answers in the wind, the earthquakes, and fire. These are all places that God is not in. He is in the still, small voice, Alex.

When you came to Jesus so many years ago, His Spirit came to reside in you. This is the still, small voice you need to follow to find what it is that you're looking for. You must **ARISE** _now Alex! It is_ **critical** _for you to make this decision. It is YOUR decision. Will you arise above your circumstances, eat and drink of God's word, and CHOOSE LIFE??? Pray now, Alex...before it's too late!!!_

Dear God, I come to You in the mighty name of Your Son, Jesus, and ask You to open my eyes, ears, heart, and spirit to understand how my life is really no different than Elijah's. Please help me to understand what I am reading, and apply the truths of Your Word to my life. Please help me to respond to Your Word. Help me learn how to hear You speaking to me with Your still, small voice...

Your son/daughter_____ Date _____

Read 1 Kings 19:1-12:

And Ahab told Jezebel all that Elijah had done, also how he had executed all the prophets with the sword. Then Jezebel sent a messenger to Elijah saying, "So let the gods do to me, and more also, if I do not make your life as the life of one of them by tomorrow about this time." And when he saw that, he arose and ran for his life, and went to Beersheba, which belongs to Judah, and left

his servant there. But he himself went a day's journey into the wilderness, and came and sat down under a broom tree. And he prayed that he might die, and said, "It is enough! Now, Lord, take my life, for I am no better than my fathers!" Then, as he lay and slept under a broom tree, suddenly an angel touched him, and said to him, "Arise and eat." Then he looked, and there by his head was a cake baked on coals, and a jar of water. So he ate and drank, and lay down again. And the angel of the Lord came back the second time, and touched him, and said, "Arise and eat, because the journey is too great for you." So he arose, and ate and drank; and he went in the strength of that food forty days and forty nights as far as Horeb, the mountain of God. And there he went into a cave and spent the night in that place; and behold, the word of the Lord came to him, and He said to him, "What are you doing here, Elijah?" So he said, "I have been very zealous for the Lord God of hosts; for the children of Israel have forsaken Your covenant, torn down Your altars, and killed Your prophets with the sword. I alone am left; and they seek to take my life." Then He said, "Go out, and stand on the mountain before the Lord." And behold, the Lord passed by, and a great and strong wind tore into the mountains and broke the rocks in pieces before the Lord, but the Lord was not in the wind; and after the wind an earthquake, but the Lord was not in the earthquake; and after the earthquake a fire, but the Lord was not in the fire; and after the fire a still, small voice.

What or who are you running from? Where are you running to? Why?

_____

_____

_____

What is God showing you about your life through this story?

_____

_____

_____

How do you think you can recognize the still, small voice in your life?

_____

_____

_____

I love you, Alex, and want the best for you. But, I can never love you like Jesus does! It is *His voice* that you need to follow. I can only point you to Him. His voice is the voice that comforts me, guides me, and sustains me when the journey gets too hard. *This still, small voice wants to do the same for you.*

You have been through a lot in your young life, Alex. Your journey has been harder than others, but not as hard as some. God has everything you need to make it through this life, but you have got to want His help. He will not force Himself on you, but keeps His arms opened wide to receive you at any time.

Isaiah 30:20-21 gives us an idea of how God, through His *still, small voice*, will guide us when we are going through tough times. Read it with me, Alex...

And though the Lord gives you the bread of adversity and the water of affliction, yet your teachers will not be moved into a corner anymore. But your eyes shall see your teachers. Your ears shall hear a word behind you, saying, "This is the way, walk in it." Whenever you turn to the right hand or whenever you turn to the left.

Believe me, Alex, the time will come when you will hear the *still, small voice*, and follow Him into your destiny! This has been my prayer for you all these years, and the Lord will do what He said He would do. Reach out to Him today! Open your heart to His *still, small voice*. Let Him teach you, guide you, and show you the way to the awesome destiny He has prepared for you!

I send my love and blessings of peace and hope to you, expecting to hear the great things God is doing in your life, as you respond to His *still, small voice*...

All my love,
Granny

* * *

I remember what happened after I read Granny's letter and responded to the *still, small voice*. It's as clear to me as if it happened yesterday...

Of course, I was locked up. I was sitting on my bunk looking out the window... well...if you can call it a window. They had covered the glass with this milky plastic-type material. I suppose we were getting too much enjoyment out of looking at the sky, who knows.

Anyhow, it was after chow and count. Most everyone was quiet doing their own thing, and we were being confined to our beds for some kind of infraction.

I was trying to do what Granny said…listen for the *still, small voice*. I didn't take much stock in the whole thing, seemed kind of *out there* to me, but, because I trusted Granny, I was willing to give it a try.

I noticed a dark spot through the milky material hovering at eye level. I got up to walk toward the spot when I heard a *still, small voice*. It was very faint, but I will never forget what I heard. *This is My beloved Son, in whom I am well pleased.*

> **I got up to walk toward the spot when I heard a *still, small voice*. It was very faint, but I will never forget what I heard.**

"What???" I said out loud. Surprised at my own voice, I looked around, hoping no one heard me.

Then I heard…*This is My beloved Son, Hear Him.*

I stopped dead in my tracks, watching this dark spot hovering outside the window. It would move up a little, then down. Then, circle around, and halt again. This went on for several minutes, and I just stood there. Then, I heard a thud as the spot hit the window.

I walked over, expecting to see the spot fall to the ground, but, amazingly it hovered in place long enough for me to catch its form. It circled around as if to tell me all is well, and then, slowly it faded from sight.

"Hudson, everything ok over there?"

"Yes Sir. Yes."

"Hudson, get back in your bunk."

"Yes Sir. Yes."

As I slowly walked back to my bunk, I heard…

It was a dove...

Now, when you're thrown into a cage with people you don't know, and most you can't figure out, you become cynical and mistrusting. I really didn't trust anybody but myself, so I kept my little *out there* episode with the dark spot and *the voice* to myself.

I swore I'd never tell anybody about it...with the exception of Granny, of course. But, I wasn't even sure about doing that. I was paranoid that if I wrote her and my letter got into the wrong hands, I'd end up in the crazy pod for the rest of my life.

It took me a couple of days, but I finally wrote and told her. I wanted to see if I would *hear* any more before I sent the letter. Well...I didn't. So, I chalked it up to a one-time experience that I probably concocted up in my sub-conscious to make her happy. After all, that's what the shrinks would say. They've told me that before. I was totally caught off guard by her response. You'd have thought I'd just won the lottery and was going to be able to set her up for life...

My dear Alex!!!!

I am thrilled beyond measure to receive your letter, and learn about the miracle God has done in your life! I am sure you have a lot of questions, so I will start by telling you...yes God was speaking to you with His still, small voice. The reason I can be certain of this, is because you were hearing <u>The Word of God</u>. *And, in two different places, I might add!!!*

You will be SO blown away when I tell you this...what you heard was SCRIPTURE!!!! I can prove it to you!!! I'm going to write the verses out here, but I want you to get your Bible, if you have one. Or, if you don't, get somebody's and read it for yourself!!!

You are at the beginning of an awesome relationship with Jesus, learning to hear His voice for yourself!!! I could not be more excited than I am right now!!! Thank You, Jesus for Your grace and mercy upon my Alex!!! Thank You, God!!!

So here goes Alex, read for yourself and BELIEVE!!!!

Matthew 3: 16-17 When He had been baptized, Jesus came up immediately from the water; and behold, the heavens were opened to Him, and He saw the Spirit of God descending like a dove and alighting upon Him. And suddenly a

voice came from heaven, saying, "This is My beloved Son, in whom I am well pleased."

Luke 9:35 And a voice came out of the cloud, saying, "This is My beloved Son. Hear Him!"

Do you understand, Alex? That *still, small voice* was showing you that *you can* and *do hear* God speaking to you! Somewhere along the line, you have heard or read those verses, and Jesus brought them back to your memory.

Read for yourself how this works…

John 14:26: But the Helper, the Holy Spirit, whom the Father will send in My name, He will teach you all things, and bring to your remembrance all things that I said to you.

Alex! This is SO EXCITING!!! Can you feel the excitement??!! Write John 14:26 out on the lines here, and pray that Jesus will bring to your remembrance more things every day…and HE WILL!!!

John 14:26:

_____

_____

_____

Read John 10:27 and see what Jesus says about this!!! Then, write it out:

John 10:27: My sheep hear My voice, and I know them, and they follow Me.

_____

_____

Now, how about making it personal by filling in the blanks with your name and then reading the statements out loud…

John 14:26 But the Helper, the Holy Spirit, whom the Father will send in Jesus' name, He will teach me, _____ all things and bring to my, _____ remembrance all things that He has said to me, _____.

John 10:27 I, _____ **am one of Jesus' sheep and I,** _____ **hear His voice, and He knows me,** _____ **and I,** _____ **follow Him.**

When you saw the spot outside your window, and heard the _still, small voice,_ Jesus was bringing back to your remembrance what you had already read or heard!!! Is that not too cool? Very exciting, indeed, my dear Alex!!!

And, it's only the beginning!!! Keep listening and keep hearing!!! Yippee!!!

All my love,
Granny

* * *

I close my eyes and listen. At first, the only thing I hear is the fire crackling.

Alex?

I lean back and smile. With a sigh of relief, I recognize the still, small voice. The Lord is gently calling my name. I've been inching away from Him, and He still calls for me!

"Yes, Lord?"

Alex, I'm taking the boredom the devil tried to re-claim you with and am using it to rescue you. When you sought refuge at Hillbilly's, I used that situation to open your eyes to what is happening to him, and to show you that you are not far behind if you don't refocus.

You're worried about a lot of things that you need to let Me handle. You spend too much time worrying about your future, when your time would be much better spent in My presence. You're trying to do this thing called life without Me.

I need to be your focus, Alex, not your future, not your worries. **My presence is what you need.** _I will fill you. I will refresh you. I will do the things in your life that destiny calls for. You've got to trust Me, Alex. I AM your destiny, Alex...you don't have to search anymore. Destiny is about a personal relationship with Me, and what we will do together to expand the kingdom of my Son._

Destiny-thieves lose their power when you are in My presence. They have no authority over your life as you seek Me and find Me. It is your choice, Alex. Who will you serve? Who will you spend time with? Who will you permit to walk with you, guide you, and control the remainder of your days?

Who will you listen to…the destiny-thieves or My still, small voice?

I give you the free will to choose. It's your choice, Alex…

Tears are running down my face as I respond to the Lord's voice. I reach over to the table beside Granny's chair and grab her Bible. This is the most amazing Bible I have ever seen. There are years and years of notes written in here. Almost every page is colorfully decorated with names, dates, and places.

Of course, there are a lot of verses with my name beside them! These are the verses I know she must have sat in this very chair, reading out loud, and pounding heaven for their fulfillment in my life. The worn and tattered pages are stained with her tears. I know her prayers have no limitations concerning time, so the fact that I am sitting here, right now, is an answer to at least one of them.

As the deer pants for the water…

The words soothe my aching heart, and allow me to become re-focused. My issues with boredom and poor choices all stem from the *vacuum in my soul* that has been created by looking everywhere else but to God for my destiny and purpose.

I was all too ready to tell Hillbilly what he needed to do with his life, when, all along, I was running on empty. I see the hypocrisy in this, and ask God to forgive me, and give me another chance with Hillbilly.

Alex, without Me you can do nothing.

"Yes, Lord."

But with Me, you can do all things.

"Yes, Lord."

Seek Me with all your heart, and you will find Me.

"Yes, Lord."

My issues with boredom and poor choices all stem from the vacuum in my soul that has been created by looking everywhere else but to God for my destiny and purpose.

Abide in Me, and I in you. As the branch cannot bear fruit of itself, unless it abides in the vine, neither can you, unless you abide in Me.

"Yes, Lord."

Peace to you! As the Father has sent Me, I also send you…

"Yes, Lord."

I stare into the fire that is warming my body, as the fire of God warms my heart. I am being transformed from the inside out. My miserably cold, dead heart is being brought back to life by the power of the Word of God.

Lazarus, come forth!

"Yes, Lord."

Alex, come forth!

"Yes, Lord."

Alex…and he who had died came out bound hand and foot with grave clothes, and his face was wrapped with a cloth. And I said to them, loose him, and let him go.

"Yes, Lord."

I get up to stir the fire and my cell phone beeps.

Man! I forgot to turn that thing down. For a minute I think about ignoring it, but the *still, small voice* says *open the text...*

Hillbilly rushed to hospital...thought you'd want to know... later...Sandusky.

Fireside Chat
Still, Small Voice

Well, I made it home without any confrontations with the law, or Mr. Sullivan and his watchdog. Even though I'm concerned about Hillbilly, I am experiencing the Lord's presence again. I know He never left me, but my awareness of His presence had been clouded. I am being revived, refreshed, and redirected.

During my deep soul-searching on the way home from Hillbilly's, I came to the conclusion that I needed to get reconnected with God, and, do it, like *NOW*. The feeling in my *gut* was that I was headed for the slammer if I didn't. I saw an old pattern try to grab hold of me, and I'm *not* about to fall into its clutches again.

Not responding to boredom and rejection in a Godly manner today led me to entertain evil thoughts, and make poor choices. Those poor choices led me to Hillbilly's, where my past came screaming back to haunt me.

After hiding out and trying my best to do something positive, I ended up running like a convicted felon. Paranoia set in, and I found myself looking behind me at the slightest noise, fearing for my freedom.

Hoping that old man Sullivan was full of hot air, and the law wasn't stalking me, was *exactly* the <u>frame of mind</u> the *evil destiny-thieves* wanted me to be in. They wanted my focus to return to my past life, with all its fears and temptations, and steer me away from the *destiny* God has prepared for me.

Let's take a minute and examine the scriptures the Lord used to get my attention while I was sitting in Granny's chair in front of the fire. I believe they will help you on your journey to wholeness, and give you the ammunition you need to defeat the *evil destiny-thieves* in your life.

Pray with me before we start:

Lord Jesus, I come to You as Your son/daughter desiring a closer relationship with You. I ask You to be with me as I meditate on the scriptures You have given Alex, and I ask that You reveal Yourself to me through them.

I am desperate for a change in my life. I am sick and tired of being sick and tired. I want to live life the way You intended me to live it. I want to seek You as my destiny, and from my relationship with You, I want to help others do the same.

I realize without You, I can do nothing. I realize that I am living in a fallen world where people will fail me whether they intend to or not. I come to You with my broken dreams, my broken heart, and ask You to help me walk into the destiny You have prepared for me.

Help me to look to You for all I need. You promised to be with me until the end of the age, to never leave me or forsake me. I ask You to remind me of these things when my mind wanders into places it shouldn't go.

Help me, God, to do Your will. Guide me, teach me, correct me, and propel me into my destiny by Your still, small voice. Thank You for loving me perfectly like only You can.

I love You Lord,

_____ name _____ date

Let's begin by declaring God's Word over our lives. We'll do this by reading the following verses and writing them out. Then, we will thank Jesus for making their truths real to us.

If at all possible, speak these statements out loud:

1. God loves me. He cares about me. He sees me when I cry. He brings me victory in my distress. Verse to meditate on and write out: Psalm 56: 8-9

You remember my wanderings; Put my tears into Your bottle; Are they not in Your book? When I cry out to You, Then my enemies will turn back; This I know because God is for me. Psalm 56:8-9

_____

_____

_____

_____

Prayer of thanksgiving : Thank You for never casting me away, even though I wander far from You. Thank You for taking my tears and making them Your own. Thank You for caring about me, and promising me victory in my distress. _____

_____

_____

Personal notes on Psalm 56:8-9:

_____

_____

2. God has given me a choice...who will I follow and serve? He says the choices I make will cause me to experience life or death. Verse to meditate on and write out: Deuteronomy 30:19-20

I call heaven and earth as witnesses today against you, that I have set before you life and death, blessing and cursing; therefore choose life, that both you and your descendants may live; that you may love the Lord your God, that you may obey His voice, and that you may cling to Him, for He is your life and the length of your days; and that you may dwell in the land which the Lord swore to your fathers, to Abraham, Isaac, and Jacob, to give them.

_____

_____

_____

_____

Prayer of thanksgiving: Thank You, Jesus, for giving me free will to choose to listen to You, and follow You. Thank You, that You love me enough to speak to me and show me Your ways. Thank You for guiding me. Thank You for helping me choose to live life in peace and harmony with You by my side. Thank You, Jesus, that You receive me today as I *choose* to follow You all the days of my life. Thank You for Your promise to bring me into my destiny, as I choose You, and cling to You. Amen.

Personal notes on Deuteronomy 30:19-20

_____

_____

_____

3. God says I cannot survive this life without His Word. Natural food may keep me alive physically, but without hearing His Word, I will die spiritually.

Verse to meditate on and write out: Matthew 4:4

But He answered and said, "It is written, 'Man shall not live by bread alone, but by every word that proceeds from the mouth of God.'"

_____

_____

Prayer of thanksgiving: Thank You, Jesus, for showing me why I am so weak spiritually. Thank You, that You want to speak to me through Your word. Please give me the desire, and time to meditate on Your Word. Teach me to listen to Your voice for guidance in order to fulfill the destiny You have planned for me.

Personal notes on Matthew 4:4:

_____

_____

_____

4. God's Word says I have the ability to hear His voice and follow Him into my destiny because I am His. Verse to meditate on and write out: John 10:27

My sheep hear My voice, and I know them, and they follow me.

_____

_____

Prayer of thanksgiving: Thank You, Jesus, that You call me Your own! Thank You, that because I am Yours, I am able to hear You and follow You into my God-given destiny. Please help me develop a listening ear by reading and meditating on Your word. Help me follow You on the path You have set out for me. Help me leave this path that I have chosen for myself, so I can be all You created me to be. Amen.

Personal notes on John 10:27:

_____

_____

_____

_____

_____

5. The Holy Spirit helps me remember everything I have read in God's Word when I need it. He is my guide, teacher, and helper in time of need. Verse to meditate on and write out: John 14:26

But the Helper, the Holy Spirit, whom the Father will send in My name, He will teach you all things, and bring to your remembrance all things that I said to you.

_____

_____

Prayer of thanksgiving: Thank You, Jesus, that You have sent The Holy Spirit to help me, guide me, and bring back to my remembrance everything You have told me. Help me to understand everything I read, and to apply it to my life. Help me to lean on You in my time of need, and be ready to hear Your voice, reminding me of what You have said. Amen.

Personal notes on John 14:26:

_____

_____

_____

Because we have chosen to follow Jesus into our destiny, He promises to speak to us about it. Please take a few minutes before we find out what's happening with Hillbilly to re-read these last five verses. Ask Jesus to speak to you about your current situation, and what He wants to do to help you move forward into your destiny in Him. Use the following lines to write what you feel He is saying to you.

Use extra paper if needed. He will continually speak to you as you seek His help!

_____

_____

_____

Let's get to the hospital and see what's going on...

Chapter 7

Hillbilly's Hope

I walk past the front desk fighting unpleasant thoughts about the receptionist. My first encounter with her was…how can I say it politely? Rather offensive. She was abrupt, uncaring, and dismissed me without so much as a hello.

Our conversation went something like this…"Can you tell me which room Samuel Cartwright's in? He might be listed as Hillbilly." Without missing a beat clicking away at her computer, she pointed to her right. "301…third floor…last room on the left…elevator's down the hall." Not once did she look up, or acknowledge me.

I take the elevator up to the third floor and walk down the hall. I pass several rooms with doors open. I see and hear things that are missing in Hillbilly's room…

…cards, balloons, visitors, conversations.

Hillbilly's been here for several weeks. To my knowledge, I'm the only visitor he's had. It's my understanding things are pretty much the same at the farm, except the place is full of people shacking up and partying all the time now. I haven't been back since the day he threw me out, even though Sandusky keeps texting me, telling me to stop by.

When I see his texts, I immediately delete them. I can't risk entertaining the thought. I need to leave my past behind in order to move into my God-given destiny. I know my trigger people and places. Sandusky's the last person I need to be around, and Hillbilly's farm is the last place I need to be.

Right now, I know the place I need to be is in this hospital by Hillbilly's side. The doctors say he has been unresponsive, and they have him hooked up to all kinds of machines with tubes.

I come every day, pull my chair right up to the edge of his bed, open my Bible, and read to him. He doesn't respond, but that doesn't keep me from doing it.

One day I heard... *Alex, he's ready. Go read to him. Tell him not to give up. His work is not finished yet.*

So, here I sit day after day, reading to my unresponsive friend, because I heard a *still, small voice* telling me to do so.

"Hillbilly...Hillbilly...It's me...Alex. Hillbilly, listen to me. Don't you go and give up on me now, Hillbilly. You got work to do. You're not finished yet. As a matter of fact, I know for certain you haven't even started. You listen here, Hillbilly. I got something real important to say to you. And, you know, old friend, you can't throw me out of here...this time you have to listen."

"Open up your heart, old friend. Listen to what God's Spirit is saying to your spirit. It is truth, Hillbilly. You and me, we got some unfinished business to tend to. We got things we need to accomplish before you and me check out of this life. Just listen, Hillbilly..."

"I'm going to read from Ephesians 2:10, Hillbilly. And, you receive it. All of it... ok?" I lean forward and whisper in his ear...

For we are God's masterpiece. He has created us anew in Christ Jesus, so we can do the good things he planned for us long ago.

"We're God's masterpieces, Hillbilly. Yeah, you and me. Can you figure that? We are His masterpieces. We are created to do good things that God planned for us to do a long time ago. Hillbilly, we both messed up our lives so bad, but not so bad that God can't straighten them out, and have us end up doing what He created us to do!!! Hillbilly, He told me to come here every day and read to you, and tell you the same thing over and over again."

"He said your spirit would receive the words, and you would understand even though we can't see any response from you. He said you and me, we have things to do, that your time was not up, for you to fight, Hillbilly. Fight to live...Hillbilly. Fight...Fight...Fight."

> **"You are His masterpiece, His workmanship, Hillbilly. He gave you life, and says it's not over yet...it has just begun."**

"You are His masterpiece, His workmanship, Hillbilly. He gave you life, and says it's not over yet...it has just begun. Hillbilly, don't' give up on me, old friend. Don't give up the fight. You still have things to do, Hillbilly...big things...things that are going to change lives. Hillbilly...don't give up! It's not your time yet!!!"

I stand and thank God for one more day to come and minister to my old friend. I ask Him to help Hillbilly receive and retain everything that was said. I ask God to heal his body so he's able to finish the assignment he's been given. I ask God to reveal Jesus to him so that he can come to salvation, and follow Jesus to the destiny He has set for him.

I reach into my pocket, pull out a jar of anointing oil, and place a dab of oil on my friend's forehead. "I stand in the gap for you my friend, and I anoint you with oil as the scriptures tell us in James 5:14. I pray the Lord God, Jehovah Rapha, that is to say, the Lord our Healer, would touch your body, mind, soul, spirit, and bring you to fullness of healing and health, to prosper you, to fulfill the destiny set before you. I pray the God of all salvation would reveal His Son Jesus to you, and that you would respond to His call to become His child this day. Amen."

I lift Hillbilly's lifeless arm and it flops down on the bed. His face is as unresponsive as his body. I walk toward the door and turn around. I'm fighting a spiritual battle. The facts I see in the natural are trying to swallow up my faith in the Lord of the supernatural.

Thoughts of hopelessness try to choke my spirit as I wave another goodbye to my motionless friend. I glance out the window before I make my exit. It is as bleak outside as it is in here. Gray skies threatening a cold rain intensify my feelings of despair.

I notice something hovering at the center of the window. Wonder what that is? I am drawn to the window for closer inspection. As I walk toward the window, my heartbeat increases with anticipation. Could it be? Really?

There, in all of its created glory, full of meaning for me...was a dove! Visions of the dove I saw years ago in the milky covered window in prison come to the forefront of my mind.

Be still and know that I am God...Be still and know that I will complete what I have started. Be still and know...

I walk back past Hillbilly's bed, and toward the door with a renewed sense of hope and peace. God is still, and always will be, the One with the last say...

Fireside Chat
Hillbilly's Hope

I don't know about you, but I've learned a whole bunch about myself and God's dealings with me since I was in the courtroom bored out of my mind.

Here's what I've learned…

1. I have finally come to realize that God is the only One who can steer me in the right direction, give me peace, and show me what will fill the huge gap in my soul.
2. I need to walk with Him every minute of every day, expecting Him to show me what I need to do, and obey what He shows me.
3. People can and will fail me, but God never will. I need to quit relying on people to fill the emptiness in my soul.
4. I have a destiny that only God can fill. I need to quit trying to find that destiny in other people, places, and things.
5. God does, and will continue to speak to me in special ways that only He and I know about. (the dove)
6. Boredom, rejection, and isolation are just some of the destiny-thieves I have encountered recently. If I am walking in my God-given destiny, boredom, rejection, and isolation will never stop me.
7. I am valuable, I am unique, and my destiny is important in the big picture.
8. I am created with special gifts and talents that my destiny requires to be fulfilled.
9. I can hear the voice of Jesus because I am His!

On the following lines, add anything you have learned in our journey so far that I have not listed: _____

_____

_____

_____

_____

There is something new happening in addition to all these things I just mentioned. I am beginning to walk in my destiny as I continue to visit Hillbilly. God has asked me to speak life-giving words to my friend, even though he doesn't respond.

We are not responsible for the results of what we do in obedience to God, He is. What we are responsible for is to do the things He asks us to do. In this case, He is asking me to keep going to visit Hillbilly, read the same verse, and say the same thing to him every day. The result is up to God, and I am not to get discouraged along the way, when I don't see the results I am expecting.

I have to believe God is working behind the scenes in Hillbilly's life. For all I know, he's better off the way he is right now, because his mind cannot argue against the Word of God, and his spirit can receive it immediately. This wouldn't be the way to do things if it was up to me, but then again, *it isn't* up to me!

Read Isaiah 55:8 and write it out on the lines following:

"For My thoughts are not your thoughts, Nor are your ways My ways," says the Lord. "For as the heavens are higher than the earth, So are My ways higher than your ways, And My thoughts than your thoughts."

_____

_____

_____

Here, God makes it clear that His plans, and the way He carries them out, are better than anything we could ever possibly think of.

I am anxious for Hillbilly to come to Jesus, get healed, and get on with this destiny thing. And, I want it to happen...like...yesterday!

I have no idea what God is doing behind the scenes, because Hillbilly does not have the ability to share anything with me. I have to trust God that what I am doing is not in vain. I have to trust God when I don't see any change. I have to believe that my part is to visit him, read the same verse, and tell him the same thing over and over again, until God says stop.

It's that simple...or is it?

Write about a time when you have been praying, and praying, and it seems like nothing is changing.

_____

_____

_____

_____

_____

Answer the following questions on the lines provided. Be honest with yourself.

Do you believe God is working behind the scenes? Are you willing to _TRUST_ Him? Have you asked Him what your part is? Are you willing to believe that His ways and thoughts are higher than yours? Why or why not?

_____

_____

_____

_____

_____

_____

Write a prayer to God asking for His help in understanding your situation, and how you are to pray, and what your part is in changing it for the better:

_____

_____

_____

_____

_____

Meditate on the prayer you just wrote, and ask God to speak to you about your situation. On the following lines, write what you believe He is saying to you: (Remember, any time God speaks to us, what He says will ALWAYS line up with what is written in the Bible.)

_____

_____

_____

_____

_____

_____

Along with realizing God's ways and thoughts are higher, (much better) than ours, we need to have the ability to *TRUST* Him when everything in the natural is in opposition to what we know is true in the spiritual.

I know that God is working in Hillbilly's life because He loves Hillbilly, and wants to see him live out his destiny *MUCH MORE* than I ever could. I have to *TRUST* God when I see no change.

Read and write out Proverbs 3:5-6

Trust in the Lord with all your heart, and lean not on your own understanding; In all your ways acknowledge Him, And He shall direct your paths.

_____

_____

There are 3 things Proverbs 3:5-6 tells us to do in order for us to be able to follow the path God has for us. Fill in the blanks:

1. _____ in the Lord with all my heart.

2. _____ on my own understanding.

3. _____ Him in all my ways.

Again, we are told not to lean on our own understanding. I believe this is because if we lean on our understanding instead of trusting God, we will surely fall.

Write about a situation where you need to trust God instead of leaning on your own understanding and ability to make things happen. Then, write a prayer asking God to help you trust him, and quit trying to do things on your own:

_____

_____

_____

_____

_____

Now...back to our story...

Chapter 8

Regret's Retaliation

I'm sitting by the fire and Ms. Madeline is out in the kitchen doing whatever it is she does out there. I don't smell any goodies baking, so she must be cleaning.

I've had a great week as far as job hunting goes, and I have a really good chance of landing a construction job. They don't care what kind of history I have, and they could care less about my list of convictions. They just need some muscles, and somebody willing to show up every day. That I can do on both accounts. I'm still pretty fit from working out, and we live on a bus route. Its seasonal work which is a bummer, but it's inside, and for that I'm eternally grateful. It's been a long winter.

On the other hand, it's *not* been such a hot week at the hospital. I'm growing weary of the same old, same old. Hillbilly lies there, the same yesterday, today, and probably tomorrow. I still go because I believe I'm supposed to. I sit and ponder these past weeks ministering to him, wondering if it's made any difference at all.

It is finished.

"Lord…is that You?"

Yes. Trust Me.

"Lord, I've done all I can do. I've read to him. I've anointed him. I've told him everything You told me to. Day after day, the same thing, and nothing's changed. He just lays there, a dead man, breathing because of a machine…."

It is finished.

"What's finished, Lord?"

Trust Me.

Here goes the blasted cell phone again.

You better get to the hospital quick…Sandusky.

Emotional adrenaline kicks in, and I yell, "Ms. Madeline its Hillbilly! I've got to get to the hospital! Pray that he hangs on till I get there…please!" I grab my coat and run as fast as I can down several blocks to the bus stop.

Whew! I stop and sit on the curb, my chest sill heaving from the marathon I just ran. I look at my watch and smile. It was a birthday present from Granny the year I turned eighteen. Of course, I had to wait till I got out of the county jail before she could give it to me. That's been the story of my life…always waiting to get out of somewhere…anyhow…it looks like I beat the bus.

Anger rises as I think about Sandusky. He must have something in the works to be so worried about Hillbilly. I heard a while back that he's hit him up several times about becoming partners or some such nonsense. This, like most of the information I receive from the street, I rejected as soon as I heard it. Now, I'm not so sure that was wise. Could there be some truth in it? Why *else* would Sandusky care *anything* about Hillbilly? Harvest Acres, if cleaned up and renovated, would be worth a boat load of cash, and we all know it.

I'm getting angrier by the minute, and that's the last thing I need to do now. Hillbilly's life is in the balance, and time is ticking. I glance down the street. Here comes the bus.

Hillbilly, hang in there! I'm on my way…

I hate public transportation. It's noisy, crowed, and you have no control over who's riding with you. However, it *is* much better than having to walk miles and miles in the freezing rain. Spring can't come soon enough for this weary, old traveler. I take a window seat, praying I get to Hillbilly in time.

I realize *real men do cry*, as I stare out the window, watching trees fly by with a lone tear making its way down my cheek. Memories of Hillbilly and all we've been through run through my mind. As most people do when they are faced with something they'd rather not deal with, I try to shut them out.

Visions of the last bus-load of kids pulling away from *Triple H* all those years ago are relentless. I hear their cries of disappointment. I see their faces in the windows, pleading for an explanation. No matter how hard I try to replace the visions with something else, they return, each time with intensity. I revisit my reaction to Hillbilly's change of character, and my inability to hold things together in a crisis.

Guilt rises up, threatening to choke me, as I envision myself standing behind the barn over Hillbilly's grave.

Now, here I sit on a bus, having to rely on public transportation, because of my inability to keep things together, and get my license back. I am overwhelmed by a sense of failure. I have failed, not only in my own life, but in the lives of those I love. I feel as though I have made no lasting, positive influence anywhere.

Guilt rises up, threatening to choke me, as I envision myself standing behind the barn over Hillbilly's grave. He made me promise to bury him there beside Sarah Jane and little Samuel if he went on before me. I can't imagine anyone else there, except maybe Ms. Madeline, because nobody wanted Hillbilly around unless they could get something from him. Tears spill over as I confront the truth.

Me and Hillbilly…we've been through too much together for it to end up like this. I should have tried harder. I should have called…even though I knew he'd curse at me and hang up. I should have showed up at the shack…whether he wanted me there or not. I should have pushed through all the invisible barriers between us. I should have been more determined…

The endless list of *I should haves* slice at my heart, one by one, with the obvious intention of mortal wounding, until I hear the bus driver announce, "Tri-County Hospital."

I follow the passengers out in a state of numbness, which I am grateful for, because feeling anything right now would be excruciatingly painful. I brace myself for what's ahead...

Fireside Chat
Regret's Retaliation

I can't think of a more deadly combination of destiny-thieves than guilt, shame, and fear. They are never far from each other, and their goal is to paralyze. They strive to move us as far away from God as they can. They do this by reminding us of past failures, and bombarding us with feelings of regret.

Regret is poison to our destiny, potent enough to kill. Regret not only tells us we have failed, but accuses us of *being a failure.* If regret is strong enough to make us believe it, we will never pursue God and our destiny. Regret truly makes mountains out of mole hills, adding false accusations to our already broken spirits.

Regret's favorite time to strike is when we are encountering God in an intimate way. It fumes and fusses because it cannot stand for us to be walking in harmony with life and God. It lies in wait and catches us off guard when we least expect it. Some of my most intense seasons of battling regret have been immediately after ministering to others, or encountering God in a special way.

These guilt, shame, and fear destiny-thieves have been around since the beginning of time. Let's take a look in Genesis to see where it all started:

Genesis 3: 1-10:

Now the serpent was more cunning than any beast of the field which the Lord God had made. And he said to the woman, "Has God indeed said, 'You shall not eat of every tree of the garden?'" And the woman said to the serpent, "We may eat the fruit of the trees of the garden; but of the fruit of the tree which is in the midst of the garden, God has said, 'You shall not eat it, nor shall you touch it, lest you die.'"

Then the serpent said to the woman, "You will not surely die. For God knows that in the day you eat of it your eyes will be opened, and you will be like God, knowing good and evil. So when the woman saw that the tree was good for food, that is was pleasant to the eyes, and a tree desirable to make one wise, she took of its fruit and ate. She also gave to her husband with her, and he ate.

Then the eyes of both of them were opened, and they knew that they were naked; and they sewed fig leaves together and made themselves coverings.

And they heard the sound of the Lord God walking in the garden in the cool of the day, and Adam and his wife hid themselves from the presence of the Lord God among the trees of the garden.

Then the Lord God called to Adam and said to him, "Where are you?" So he said, "I heard Your voice in the garden, and I was afraid because I was naked; and I hid myself."

Re-read Genesis 3:1-10 and answer the following questions:

What does the serpent (the devil) do in order to get the woman to do the wrong thing?

_____

_____

_____

What is the woman's reaction to the serpent's (the devil's) suggestions?

_____

_____

_____

What happens to the man and the woman after they listen to the serpent's (devil's) suggestions?

_____

_____

_____

After Adam and Eve disobeyed God, guilt, shame, and fear entered their lives. They were exposed. They tried to cover themselves and hide from God.

Has this ever happened to you? Write about a time when you felt exposed and you experienced guilt, shame, and fear:

_____

_____

What did you do to try to cover yourself and hide from God?

_____

_____

What was the outcome of your efforts?

_____

_____

Friend, Jesus came to set us free from our Genesis 3 stories! He took our punishment on the cross to set us free from guilt, shame, and fear. We do not have to be afraid and try to hide from God because of what Jesus has done for us.

He says, *Fear not! It is finished! I took the blame, so you are blameless. I took the stripes so you can be free. You do not have to be a prisoner of guilt, shame, and fear, because your sins are washed away in My blood, and you are Mine!*

When guilt, shame, and fear try to paralyze you; run to Jesus. He's waiting with open arms to receive you and set you free to follow your God-ordained destiny.

Read and write out John 10:10:

The thief does not come except to steal, and to kill, and to destroy. I have come that they may have life, and that they may have it more abundantly.

_____

_____

We all have Genesis 3 stories. We all have disobeyed God, have failed family and friends, and have experienced guilt, shame, and fear. Romans 3:23 tells us that we have all sinned and fallen short of the glory of God. Guilt, shame, and fear are the results of the work of the master thief in our lives. His main goal is to stop us from fulfilling our destiny.

The thief does not come except to steal, and to kill, and to destroy.

Jesus has given us the choice to choose His remedy for our Genesis 3 stories. As we repent of our disobedience, He promises to give us abundant life, free of guilt, shame, and fear. This is the work of the Master Giver in our lives Whose desire is to guide us into our destiny. Forgiveness is His gift...

Jesus has come that we may have life, and have it more abundantly.

Will you revisit your Genesis 3 experience you wrote about earlier and ask Jesus to forgive you for trying to cover yourself and hide from Him? Will you ask Him to set you free from the guilt, shame, and fear that you experienced because of it?

Write a prayer of repentance and thanksgiving for being set free from your Genesis 3 story.

_____
_____
_____
_____
_____
_____
_____
_____
_____
_____
_____
_____
_____
_____
_____
_____
_____

Don't let guilt, shame, and fear rule your life!
Don't let regret rob you from your God-ordained destiny!
Overcome *regret's retaliation* with Jesus' gift of forgiveness!

Chapter 9

Fruit of Faithfulness

I'm about one block from the hospital now. I pull my coat sleeves over my hands. In my haste to leave the house, I forgot my gloves, and the temperature's falling fast. Only for Hillbilly would I venture out in this brutal weather.

As I walk, I'm reminded of a day when he did the same. It was years ago. Hillbilly was at Granny's shoveling her car out. We had a snowstorm the day before, and Granny wanted to get out so she could come visit me at the County jail.

I told her on the phone not to worry about it. I'd see her next week. But, no, she wouldn't hear it. Granny wasn't the swearing kind, so she said, "Alex, come *heck* or high water, I'm going to be there promptly at 3pm. You wait and see."

And, sure enough, she was. And, sure enough, it was because of Hillbilly. When she called him for help, he said, "Granny, only for Alex would I venture out in this brutal weather." What goes around, comes around, they say.

I pass the front desk where Ms. Personality sits, and feel a tug in my spirit that I should repent of my evil thoughts and greet her. That's going to have to wait. I want to get to Hillbilly before its too late…

The elevator is taking forever, it seems. Thankfully, there's no one in here I have to make idle conversation with. I exit, only to hear voices down the hall near Hillbilly's room, and see people rushing in and out.

Oh! No! No! Jesus, No! My heart races and my spirit sinks as I run down the hall. There are doctors and nurses conversing outside Hillbilly's room with looks on their faces that I can't read.

"Everybody clear out!"

I'm almost at his door when I hear my name called.

"Are you Alex Hudson?"

I'm greeted by a nurse who is clearly shaken. I nod. "Yes, M'am."

"Does Mr. Cartwright have any next of kin that you know of?"

"No, M'am." I feel like collapsing.

"We have a...a situation in there that defies explanation." She looks at what appears to be a patient chart. I assume it has notes about Hillbilly on it.

Doctors and nurses are filing out of Hillbilly's room. "Unbelievable, unlike anything I've ever seen. I thought Aunt Elsie was nuts." They brushed past me, laughing and shaking their heads. Clearly, they were unaware of my presence.

What are they talking about? I'm getting anxious, and about to lose it. This is no way to speak of the dead...no way at all. Granny would be appalled. Hillbilly, in his worst days, wouldn't show this amount of disrespect!

"M'am?" I fight unwanted anger rising within me. "Can you please tell me what's going on here? How did you know my name?"

"He told me." She pointed to Hillbilly's room and walked away.

"He who?" She doesn't answer and keeps walking.

I take a deep breath and enter Hillbilly's room. I better not find Sandusky hovering over my friend. I might just end up leaving here in handcuffs. This *truly* is one unstable, creepy hospital, if you ask me.

I walk in and scan the room. It's just as I suspected. No balloons. No cards. No doctors or nurses, they all just marched down the hall. No Sandusky…*at least I know I won't leave here in cuffs.* No nothing. Even his roommate's bed is vacant.

So, what's that noise? It's coming from behind the curtain that separates Hillbilly from his roommate. It sounds like…*slurping?* I can't think of anybody that would take the time to come see Hillbilly here, much less stay here and eat while he lays there lifeless.

Better double check…"Sandusky, that you?"

"Nope."

I pull the curtain back, and stand there as if I'd just been turned into a pillar of salt. With the biggest grin I've ever seen on any human face, Hillbilly looks up from a bowl of chicken broth and says, "Hey, Hudson. What took you so long?"

"Hudson! Why you just standing there? Come, sit by old Hillbilly." He puts his spoon down on the tray and pats the side of his bed.

> **"I seen your Man, Hudson. Really, Jesus, I mean, I been with Him."**

"I got a heap of stuff to tell you. Been *lights out* for me for a while, I know, but I been places, Hudson. I seen your Man, Hudson. Really, Jesus, I mean, I been with Him. And…He showed me a *bunch* of cool stuff, Hudson."

I'm too shocked to move.

"C'mon, Hudson. Come sit by your old friend. I'm serious, man. Don't look so freaked out. I'm not gonn'a throw you out'a here like I did at my place. I'm done with all that mess. I'm telling you straight up, Hudson…I'm done with it all. I was crazy then…not now. This is a *new creation* you're looking at, my friend."

I walk over to Hillbilly and sit like he asks. I am dumbfounded. When answered prayer is staring us in the face, why are we so surprised? As soon as I sit by Hillbilly, the Presence of the Lord surrounds us.

We grab each other in a bear hug. Hillbilly is skin and bones because of the abuse his body has endured over the years. I have no doubt, as I embrace my long-time friend, that this is a new beginning for both of us, and that he will get stronger day by day.

"Look a 'here, Hudson." Hillbilly hands me a piece of paper with *Hillbilly's House of Hope* written on the top. "It's a recovery house for addicts and their families."

When answered prayer is staring us in the face, why are we so surprised?

I'm impressed. The sketches are as if an experienced architect had drawn them. It is truly amazing.

"It's the new Triple H, Hudson. Jesus showed it to me when I was in *lights out*. Me and Him, we went walking by the Jordan River, and He gave me all kinds of ideas. Hudson, we're gon'a clean up the farm and rebuild Triple H, cept'in it's gon'a have the new name. He gave me the new name Hudson...its *Hillbilly's House of Hope*."

"The people here, the docs and the nurses, they think I'm crazy, and that I'm gon'a relapse into the old Hillbilly. No dice, Hudson. This here man has walked with The Master, and has been given marching orders to clean my place up like He cleaned me up. Make it and me useful to Him. And, you's gon'a hep me do it, Hudson, y'hear?!"

"The lady that called you by name believes me, Hudson. She's the only one. She isn't like the others who don't believe. Hudson, she said you can take me home soon. I signed the papers. It'll be a couple days. They want to watch me, see if I don't slip back into lala land. But, you and me, we know that ain't gon'a happen."

"Sandusky, he's been snooping around, checking my bank and such. He thinks I don't know, but I do. You don't need to worry about that none, Hudson. He ain't pulled the wool over my eyes no how...Jesus, the Master seen to that."

"What you got'a do now, Hudson, is look up all the Triple H kids from before. You know, the ones we taught after school. They's all got to be married, working, and have families by now. The Master's told me some of them are real good business people now, teachers, counselors, and everything we need for *Hillbilly's House of Hope*. The Master told me they'll come help us for free."

"Hillbilly, did Jesus tell you what to do about Carlucci, Sandusky, and all the mess that's going on in the barn?"

"Yeah…Hudson. Ain't gon'a be no problem. They're just gon'a leave. After the D.A. gets done with Carlucci, he'll be going down the road, and the rest of them are all gon'a run. He's the one who calls all the shots, you know that. Sandusky's in hot with him, owes him a wad, and Carlucci's thugs know it. That's why he's been snooping around, trying' to rip me off. *He's* probably on the run by now. I'm telling ya…Hudson…soon as you go back to the farm, they're all gon'a be gone."

I get up to leave and stretch my fist out to this amazing *new creation* of the Lord's. He lifts his boney right hand toward me. We tap our fists together in our knuckle pact that has been known to seal any deal we've ever made.

"Oh, and, Hudson…one more thing. Jesus done told me, we's got'a start praying for Carlucci and all of them, just like you been prayin' for me. He told me they's gon'a be helpin' us someday too."

Now it's me with the biggest grin known to man.

"Later, Hillbilly."

"Later, Hudson."

"Hillbilly…one more thing…"

"Yeah, Hudson?"

I turn away so he can't see me losing it.

"Sarah Jane, little Samuel, and Harrison would be mighty proud, my friend."

I walk out with tears dripping down my cheeks, realizing God has been working behind the scenes all along, and, my ministry to Hillbilly was never in vain.

Fireside Chat
Fruit of Faithfulness

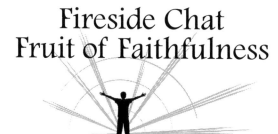

The bus ride home is just as noisy, crowed, and unappealing as ever, but I am happier than I've been in all my life. No drug, sex, or amount of money could give me the satisfaction, and sense of fulfillment I feel right now. Hillbilly's found Jesus! He's leaving his miserable past behind and walking toward his destiny. Jesus has shown him he was *created* for *so much more*!!!

The thundering noise in the bus is no match for the *still, small voice* I've come to recognize and listen to...

Alex, you did what I asked, and left the rest up to Me. Even when you felt like giving up, you rose above those feelings, and trusted Me. Now you've seen what I can do with simple trust. It's all about timing, Alex... My perfect timing.

A few verses come to mind as I meditate on what the Lord's saying. Take time to meditate on them *for yourself*, ask Him to speak to *you* about *your life*. Write what *you hear* the still, small voice saying *to you* on the lines provided.

Those who live only to satisfy their own sinful nature will harvest decay and death from that sinful nature. But those who live to please the Spirit will harvest everlasting life from the Spirit. Galatians 6:8 (Life Recovery Bible)

_____

_____

_____

_____

_____

_____

_____

_____

_____

_____

So let's not get tired of doing what is good. At just the right time we will reap a harvest of blessing if we don't give up. Galatians 6:9 (Life Recovery Bible)

_____
_____
_____
_____
_____
_____
_____

Trust in the Lord with all your heart. And lean not on your own understanding; In all your ways acknowledge Him, and He shall direct your paths. Proverbs 3:5-6

_____
_____
_____
_____
_____
_____
_____

Chapter 10

Destiny's Dedication

It's dedication day and people are buzzing around all over the place. It's been exactly one year since I brought Hillbilly home from the hospital, and, what's been done with this place would cause any home-makeover show some serious competition.

I walk over to the renovation exhibit which is set up just before you enter the house. It's amazing what God has done here since the day I hid from Mr. Sullivan and his watchdog. He has taken a filthy, drug infested barn, and turned it into a house of restoration and hope. It's not just amazing...it's miraculous.

The first picture in the exhibit shows what Hillbilly and I found right after he came home from the hospital. It was just as he said it would be. The place was vacant. Everybody split. That was good news. But, at the same time, we realized, if there was any hope of restoration, we had to deal with what they had left behind.

The place was unfit for life of any kind, animal or human. It was full of garbage. Filthy, musty mattresses lay between dirty sheets that hung from the rafters. I felt a wave of nausea come over me. We knew the sheets were hung there in an attempt to provide privacy from things no human should engage in. Drug paraphernalia, broken bottles, cards and dice were lying all over the place. Signs of young children...baby dolls and little John Deere trucks...invaded our already sickened souls. Hillbilly fell to his knees, sobbing, holding his head in his hands.

"Hudson!" He cried. "You mean to tell me I let all this here go on right under my nose for *over twenty years*?!?"

" Hillbilly…" I said. "It just happened. They took advantage of you when you were weak. You were out of your mind between grief and moonshine. It's all behind you now. God's forgiven you. He's going to do something great here in the middle of all this mess Hillbilly, I know it. He showed you His plans, remember? You showed them to me in the hospital. You just wait and see."

"Yeah, Hudson. *Hillbilly's House of Hope.* Look around here, Hudson. Don't look like much hope for this place, if'n you ask me. Ain't a dumpster big enough in the whole world to get rid of all this."

"Hillbilly, don't go letting what you see send you back into the pit of darkness. God showed you His plans…He'll make it happen…all we got to do is *trust Him.* Let's forget the past, and move on to what we know we're supposed to do with this place. We got to get busy. C'mon, Hillbilly, no use thinking of all that."

Hillbilly walks over to the renovation exhibit and stands beside me. "Here they come, Hudson." He says, and points down the road. "Let's go greet them."

Here comes a school bus, full of men and women who have donated their time, talents, and resources to help make this day happen. My heart skips a beat, and tears threaten to expose my inner emotions as I watch the bus coming toward me.

Memories of the day Hillbilly entered darkness, and *Triple H* ceased to exist, come to the front of my mind. This is the *same road,* and the *same time of day* I looked into their disappointed eyes, pleading for an explanation, so many years ago. I stood here, in this very *same spot,* watching the activity bus disappear, as the vision of *Triple H* faded away before my very eyes.

"Awe, Mr. Hudson." I can still hear their cries.

This time my heart is ready to burst because of happiness instead of sorrow. Yes, this is the *same road,* the *same time of day,* and the *same bus,* carrying the *same kids.*

Except…it is twenty-one years later. Hillbilly is at my side, not hiding in my office full of grief and moonshine. The *Triple H* kids are in their thirties. They're riding *the same bus* they were twenty years ago. Except, this time, they are *coming back* to be part of *Hillbilly's House of Hope*, not leaving *Triple H.*

The crowd gathers as Hillbilly and I walk beside the bus carrying our thirty-plus year old *Triple H* kids. They're hanging out the windows, stretching their arms toward us. Hillbilly and I reach out our palms and high-five them. We all laugh like a bunch of high-energy, high-school kids. Everyone senses excitement in the air.

As the bus slows to a halt, I scan the crowd. People from all over the county are here to celebrate with us. Most of them are volunteers that just showed up one day. *Hillbilly's House of Hope* ended up on the news one night, and from that point on, we had more help than we knew what to do with.

> **Because of what we did at Triple H, these kids became successful men and women, and leaders in our communities.**

Loud cheers erupt from the crowd as the men and woman exit the school bus. Hillbilly and I stand in awe. Because of what we did at *Triple H*, these kids became successful men and women, and leaders in our communities. We couldn't be more proud.

"Distinguished guests, volunteers, friends, and family, we have set up a tour of the house for you to enjoy before the dedication ceremony. We have done this in order for you to be able to appreciate what has been accomplished here. The farm has been restored from a place of darkness and despair to a place of refuge and hope."

"The men and women who are hosting the tour came to the farm years ago when it was an after-school program called *Triple H.* They have donated their time, talents, and resources to help make Hillbilly's hospital vision come true. Please welcome the *Triple H.* alumni…"

More cheers and clapping fill the air as our *Triple H.* kids bow and enter the house. The tour is a huge success. I hear people talking about what they learned on their way out, and it's all good. Words like…amazing, unbelievable, astonishing, and simply incredible fill the air.

As the saying goes, a picture is worth a thousand words, and in this case, probably a million. We have a framed picture of what the area looked like before it was restored hanging on each door, along with a bronze plaque naming the person the room is dedicated to.

There are twenty *restoration rooms*, one room for every year Hillbilly lost the farm to personal grief and hopelessness. These rooms are where our residents will receive healing from the past and hope for a better future. Every resident will have a mentor who will stay with them through the process. Each room is dedicated to someone special who's helped Hillbilly heal and move on, and is vital to the resident successfully making it to graduation.

We expect church leaders, community leaders, business leaders, and exceptional employees of all occupations to come from this room.

Between the *restoration rooms*, and the *graduation room*, is our *excavation room*. This *destiny-building* room is constructed over the site where all the *destiny-destroying* activity once went on in the barn. It celebrates the *excavation* of all the garbage and debris we removed in order to begin restoration. This is the place where residents will be encouraged to pursue their destiny by *excavating* their gifts and talents. We expect church leaders, community leaders, business leaders, and exceptional employees of all occupations to come from this room.

The kitchen and dining area have been constructed in the *very same* place Carlucci brought his pizza to the *Triple H.* kids the day Hillbilly lost his will to live. We have dedicated these rooms to Mrs. Carlucci who has lost both son and husband to *the system*, and believes one day they will be part of our program.

The children's wing is especially moving. It is dedicated to saving families. Here, the residents will interact with their children, learn parenting and anger resolution skills, and how to live as a family unit. I watch as men and women alike weep at the picture on the door. It's a picture of the doll and John Deere tractor we found in the middle of broken bottles, syringes, and filthy mattresses...the scene that dropped Hillbilly to his knees. The children's wing is dedicated to Sarah Jane and little Samuel, the family Hillbilly loved and lost.

The *graduation room* is where graduation ceremonies will take place as the residents complete our program. *Graduation* celebrates more than completion of a program; it *celebrates* leaving the old life behind, and pursuing the new. Today, Hillbilly is the first graduate. This room is dedicated to his vision- Giver, destiny-Maker, and best Friend...Jesus Christ of Nazareth.

As the last of the guests complete the tour, we are preparing for the dedication ceremony outside. Hillbilly has created an off-the-chain sign for the house, which we had to hire a crane operator to place for us. He is due here any minute.

Hillbilly heads for the dedication stage, which he's designed and built. He cut up some trees on the back of the property and made his own lumber. He's becoming quite the wood worker since we started this project, fulfilling part of his destiny. He built a nice sized shop, and designed the dedication stage from there. We hope to use the shop to help talented residents learn a trade that will lead them into a satisfying and successful career.

Hillbilly raises his hand to get everybody's attention, and the crowd quiets down. "Hey, y'all... Alex and me...well...we's mighty happy y'all are here to share this special day with us. Y'all know I'm not much for public speakin', but Alex here, asked me to say a few words before we get started."

"So...here I am...saying a few words."

"Hey, Hillbilly, you go on now!" Someone yells.

"Yeah...well...OK. Y'all know I been out'a sorts for a long time, and this here place got taken over by the devil, himself. He almost kilt me, he did. But, one day God saw fit to rescue me, by lettin' one of the devil's cronies find me knocked out on the floor. I was lying in my own blood, split my head wide open. Can't tell you how it happened, 'cause, you know, old Hillbilly, I was snockered."

"Anyhow, one day I woke up in the hospital with pictures of this here house stuck in my mind. Everything you's lookin' at, from the inside out. It was making me crazy. I couldn't figure it out. Then, all of a sudden, I remembered. I was in la-la land, you know, the docs call it a coma. A Man came to me and said, "C'mon Samuel, let's walk together. Yeah, He used my real name. I bet none of y'all here know that's my real name, 'ceptin' maybe Alex, here, and, of course... the law..."

A few snickers from the crowd don't throw Hillbilly off balance. He continues...

"So I said, 'Who are you?'"

"He said, 'I am Jesus, follow Me.'"

"So, I did. Just like that. Got up and followed Him. He took me to some really nasty places...people strung out on drugs, gangs running wild, old broken down buildings, full of filth...looked like old Hillbilly's barn not too long ago. Anyhow, He, this Man Who called Himself Jesus, He said to me, 'You will provide a place of refuge and healing for these people.'"

"I looked at Him like...what? Then, He showed me places where little kids had real bad things done to them, and I started to weep...Yeah...old, hard-hearted Hillbilly sobbing like a baby. Then the Man said, 'You will provide a place of refuge and healing for these children.' "

"But," I said. "How can that happen? You don't know nothing about me, you don't know what old Hillbilly's like."

"Then, this Man, He started to sing...Amazing grace how sweet the sound...'"

"Now, I'm tellin' ya'll that 'bout freaked me out...soon as He started singin' Amazing grace...I *knew* who He was. He wasn't just some guy who lived a long time ago in an old fairy tale. Cuz, only one other person in the whole world knows about that song, and I wasn't speaking to him at the time. Only the *real Jesus* would know about that...now, I'm only supposed to be sayin' a few words, so's I can't get into all that now, but I'm tellin' y'all..."

"This was the real deal, man!! This was Jesus, *The real* Jesus. All's I could do was say...You are the Lord... forgive old Hillbilly for how I been, for not knowin' You. Help me, Lord. I'm no good, I need You. I'm nothin' without You. Teach Me, Jesus. Lead me, and I'll follow." Then, I fell on my face and said, "And, if'n You can do something with old Hillbilly's life, it's Yours."

"He took me to a grassy hill and said, 'Samuel, sit with Me.' So, I sat. And, that's where He told me about *Hillbilly's House of Hope*. He drew the plans on a piece of paper and held them up against my head. He leaned over, breathed on me, and said, 'Receive your destiny.' Then He disappeared, and I woke up."

He bows and walks off the stage.

A Holy hush comes over the crowd. I get up to speak. I scan their faces. There's no denying what Hillbilly's just shared. The evidence is too strong. We are witnesses to the truth. Through *Hillbilly's House of Hope*, he will be providing a place of refuge and hope just like Jesus told him he would.

"At this time, I would like to invite all the *Triple H* men and women to the stage, for the unveiling and placement of the sign that will testify to the restoration power of Jesus, and proclaim the destiny of this building…"

The Holy hush continues as the crowd is well aware of the intense emotion this moment is bringing to all who are in involved. The *Triple H* men and women line up between Hillbilly and me, waiting for Christopher's crane to lift the sign that took Hillbilly months to create.

The Holy hush continues as the crowd is well aware of the intense emotion this moment is bringing to all who are in involved.

Hillbilly's work is…well…I am speechless. There are no words to describe what I see as the newly acceptable tears flow. In slow motion, the crane strains to lift the life-sized sign, and move it toward the top of the barn. It sways in the breeze, and we gasp, holding our breath.

We've been told Christopher is the best crane operator in the area, and I'm silently praying our information is correct. Hillbilly and I personally climbed 32ft ladders last week to attach steel brackets to the outside of the barn, so he could set the sign down on them. The brackets were custom-made, and guaranteed to hold the weight of Hillbilly's sign.

The wind picks up and Christopher has to back the crane away from the barn. Any unexpected shift; and our custom-made windows would be history. Dark clouds build on the horizon, adding to our anxiousness.

Mrs. Carlucci and her staff are working hard in the kitchen to provide us with an after-dedication celebration of their prize-winning pizza and Italian dishes. Hillbilly wanted everything to be restored from that last day with *Triple H*, including Carlucci's pizza. He checked it out, and, now that Tony and his dad are locked up, Mrs. Carlucci's calling the shots and the business is totally legit.

We stare, motionless, along with the crowd, as the crane slowly lowers the sign onto the brackets. I hear a crack, and, for a minute, my heart sinks.

All eyes are on the crane, waiting. The wind calms, and Christopher moves closer to the barn. We stare, motionless, along with the crowd, as the crane slowly lowers the sign onto the brackets. I hear a *crack*, and, for a minute, my heart sinks.

Christopher looks over to Hillbilly and me, two thumbs up, and backs away. The *crack* must have been coming from the crane as he released its hook from the sign.

There it is! Safe and sound on the top of the barn! Each letter beautifully carved, big as life, shouting to the world the restoration power of Hillbilly's Lord...

HILLBILLY'S HOUSE OF HOPE...
A PLACE OF RESTORATION AND DESTINY
FOR ALL AGES

The silent, anxious atmosphere explodes into a New Years Eve-type event. People are jumping up and down, throwing confetti, twirling around like fools, falling on the ground, shouting, "Hillbilly you've outdone yourself. Who would have known you had it in you? Where you been hiding all these years?" High-fives are going on all over the place, and Hillbilly's getting tons of business deals for work.

Somebody shouts, "Hey, Hudson. I heard Mrs. Carlucci's inside making some of her out-a-this-world, weight-gaining, mouth-watering chow. That true?"

"Yeah...You heard right." By now, it's almost impossible to hear myself talk. "Hey! Everybody! Can I have your attention? Hey! QUIET...PLEASE!!!"

"Hillbilly and I want to invite you to share our first meal with us at *Hillbilly's House of Hope* one hour from now in the dining hall. Until then, please feel free to walk the grounds. The path starts at the back of the barn and ends up at the fishing pond. You will be walking the same path the *Triple H.* kids took twenty-one years ago, the day *Triple H.* ceased to exist."

"Please take time to read the plaques we have set up along the path as you enjoy the music we have playing through our outdoor sound system. These plaques celebrate the lives of some of the kids who were with us that day. If you follow the path to the end, you will end up at the fish pond. There is a path that goes out from the fish pond, but stops in the middle of the woods. This is where we believe Mrs. Carlucci's son walked off, and left the kids."

"Hillbilly and Carlucci both sank into darkness that day. Today we celebrate Hillbilly's comeback and pray for Carlucci's. Hillbilly dedicates this entire place, first, to Jesus Christ, without Whom there would be no comeback, no vision, and no House of Hope, and then to all who would come through these doors seeking healing and hope. To God be the glory…great things He has done! We'll see you in an hour!"

Mrs. Carlucci puts the finishing touches on the tables, as her staff fills the water goblets. We have gone all out for this celebration. No paper plates and soda cans this time! Talk about restoration!

We've chosen to furnish the dining room with round tables that will seat eight guests each. I've had more than my share of sitting at large, long tables, especially if it's in a noisy place. It's a real drag. You can't hear people at the other end, and you have to yell across the room just to get some salt and pepper. We didn't want our guests to have this same unpleasant experience.

The dinner is buffet- style. Mrs. Carlucci has outdone herself. The aroma in the room is so inviting, I'm tempted to pull up a seat and gorge before the guests arrive. Thankfully, there are no utensils in the warming trays yet, keeping me from embarrassing myself.

The guests file in chattering about the events of the day. Mrs. Carlucci enters the room. "Dinner is served." Hillbilly prays over the food, and we line up antici- pating her incredibly appetizing feast.

The guests are clearly impressed. "Amazing…unbelievable! Did you read those plaques on the trail? What about that sign Hillbilly made? Who would have ever thought something so tragic could turn out so full of hope? I want to be part of what's going on here." On and on they went…

Hillbilly and I and look at each other. "Got no words, Hudson, no words." I nod in agreement. We take our seats at the front table with our *Triple H.* kids, and soak it all in.

"We've come full circle, Hillbilly, you and me, full circle."

"Yeah, Hudson, we sure have."

Hillbilly and I walk over to the exit door, and stand like pastors at the end of a Sunday church service.

Mrs. Carlucci enters and holds a water goblet in the air. "Here's a toast to *Hillbilly's House of Hope*, and to those you have created this wonderful place for. May your doors never close. I pray Mr. Carlucci, and my son Antonio will someday come here for help... cheers."

We stand as a thunderous sound of applause echoes through the room. "Thank you, Mrs. Carlucci for that, and for the off-the-charts dinner you cooked up! May your business thrive, and serve us mouth-watering Italian dishes for years to come!"

My emotions are raw as this unbelievably, incredible day ends. Hillbilly and I walk over to the exit door, and stand like pastors at the end of a Sunday church service. Hillbilly speaks as the guests get ready to leave...

"Me and Hudson, we're sure mighty happy y'all been here with us this special day. Thanks for comin' around and makin' us feel so important. Don't be strangers y'all, come by ever' once in a while, and don't ever forget what y'alls seen here today."

Hillbilly stands by a box of hand-crafted plaques he made out of scrap wood left over from the house sign. He wanted every guest to remember this day, and what it stands for.

"Hudson," he told me. "I'm gon'a make every one of them different...I mean all shapes and sizes, 'cause God made us all different. But, Hudson, every one of them plaques is gon'a have the same words on 'em. 'Cause God created us all for so much more. That's what Hillbilly's House of Hope is all about, Hudson."

"So, Hillbilly, what are you going to put on the plaques?"

"Hudson, they're gon'a say,"

NEVER GIVE UP!
BECAUSE GOD CREATED YOU
FOR SO MUCH MORE.

Fireside Chat
Destiny's Dedication

"Hudson?"

"Yeah, Hillbilly?"

"You done pretty good for someone who don't know the first thing 'bout writin' a book."

"Yeah, Hillbilly. Guess you're probably right."

"No probably 'bout it, Hudson. I *know* I'm right."

* * *

Ordinary people do extraordinary things when they embrace their God-ordained destinies. Simple shepherds slay giants, drug dealers turn houses of horror into houses of hope, and ex-cons write inspirational books. Ordinary men become fathers to the fatherless, communities are rebuilt, and history is changed.

Much of the material that breathed life into *Help! I'm Locked up...and Created for So Much More!* came from the lives of two such people...an ordinary man and woman with a barn, a horse, a donkey, and a heart for underprivileged children.

Cowboy Bill and Ms. Bonny, founders of Lazy B's Ranch in Cement City, Michigan (http://www.lazybsranch.org), are authentic examples of ordinary people doing extraordinary things as they embrace their God-ordained destinies. Lazy B's Ranch, founded in 2006, began as a tiny spark in the heart of these two simple shepherds destined to slay inner-city giants.

Their desire was to provide a safe environment in the country where children could be mentored and learn positive ways of dealing with life's challenges. Using Andy Andrew's book, *The Young Traveler's Gift*, as their curriculum and the animals as their vehicle to implement the program, the tiny spark was ignited.

Hundreds of children have come through the doors of Lazy B's Ranch and have been given a strong foundation for a positive future as they learn how to interact with each other, make good choices, and seek their destinies. Cowboy Bill and Ms. Bonny have dedicated their lives, their home, and all they own to the ranch and the kids. Jackson County, Michigan is a better place because of Lazy B's Ranch.

On January 31, 2015, with friends and family surrounding him, Cowboy Bill was called home by the One who gave him his giant-slaying ability. Heaven met earth, and earth met heaven as this father to the fatherless was ushered into the presence of Jesus. As we mourn the loss of our beloved friend who has touched so many lives, we dedicate ourselves to continue his work and celebrate what we have gained by knowing him.

As we mourn the loss of our beloved friend who has touched so many lives, we dedicate ourselves to continue his work and celebrate what we have gained by knowing him.

Standing room only was Ms. Bonny's desire. Seated in the front row, I turned to look at the clock. It was almost time to start. A sea of people from all walks of life waited to enter the room through a clogged entrance door. It was time to start and they were still coming. It was past time to start and they were still coming. I smiled as I saw people leaning against walls and sitting on tables that showcased the life of our friend; there were no more seats.

Lazy B's Ranch kids milled around the crowded room searching for comfort. I came across three of them huddled together with tears streaming down their faces. Cowboy Bill would have been so proud…one of his young men holding two of his young ladies, with a fatherly embrace that said, *I share your pain.*

Raw emotion gripped everyone as the teens voluntarily shared what Lazy B's Ranch, Ms. Bonny, and Cowboy Bill meant to them. We were standing on holy ground, and I knew it. The tiny spark that began in 2006 had grown into a full-blown flame, and Cowboy Bill's legacy will live on for generations to come.

At the beginning of this book, we talked about our lives being a poem that people can read. When God calls you home, what kind of legacy will you leave behind? What kind of seeds will you have planted? Will you have embraced your God-ordained destiny? What will people hear when *your* poem is read?

Please join me in celebrating what God can do with one ordinary man who fulfills his God-ordained destiny. I stood in front of the crowded room and read...

Welcome Home

Welcome home, My Bill, My precious son,
Your work on earth is truly done.
You've run your race, you've won the prize.
Now take My hand, My son, and rise.

Let's take a walk so you can see.
Just what it is you've done for Me.
You've plowed your field with love and care,
Planting seeds of life everywhere.

A father to the fatherless,
There is no greater call than this.
You've taken in My girls and boys,
And turned their sorrows into joys.

It was My heart that you embraced,
To give them love and such a place.
Your life lives on in those you've touched.
I've seen it all and thank you much.

You've done all that I've asked you to.
There is no more for you to do…

So welcome home My precious son.
Your work on earth is truly done.
You've run your race, you've won the prize.
Now take My hand, My son, and rise.

IN LOVING MEMORY OF BILL LIVERNOIS
December 30, 1948–January 31, 2015

A Special Note from Ms. Lynn

It is my desire to provide copies of this workbook to men and women who are in jail or prison at no charge if they feel they would benefit from its contents. To request a free copy of *Help! I'm Locked Up…and Created for So Much More!* or to get information on how to sponsor a book for someone in need, please fill out the form below and mail it to:

Lynn Potter • P.O. Box 11 • York, SC 29745

Or e-mail lynnpotter222@yahoo.com

Name _____

Address _____

_____

_____

_____

What are the guidelines for receiving books at the particular institution you are requesting *Help! I'm Locked Up…and Created for So Much More!* to be sent to?

_____

_____

_____

____ I would like to request a free book.
____ I would like more information on how to sponsor a book.
(Please supply contact information)

_____

_____

_____

Comments: Please tell me a little about yourself and your interest in this book:

_____

_____

_____

Requests for free books will be filled as sponsors become available.

Made in the USA
Charleston, SC
04 September 2015